PRETENDERS
The Isle Of View

Photos by Eugene Adebari

ISBN 0-7935-6080-2

7777 W. BLUEMOUND RD. P.O. BOX 13819 MILWAUKEE, WI 53213

Copyright © 1996 by HAL LEONARD CORPORATION
International Copyright Secured   All Rights Reserved

For all works contained herein:
Unauthorized copying, arranging, adapting, recording or public performance is an infringement of copyright.
Infringers are liable under the law.

PRETENDERS
The Isle Of View

Lyrics 8

Sense of Purpose 11
Chill Factor 18
Private Life 22
Back On The Chain Gang 27
Kid 35
I Hurt You 40
Criminal 45
Brass In Pocket 49
2000 Miles 53
Hymn To Her 58
Lovers Of Today 61
The Phone Call 69
I Go To Sleep 74
Revolution 78

Guitar Parts 87

PRETENDERS

A whole new perspective on the songs and significance of the Pretenders comes into focus on The Isle Of View, the group's eighth album in 15 years and a startling stylistic change-up from a band known for routinely defying expectations.

14 classic Pretenders tracks—ranging from such perennials as "Brass In Pocket," "2000 Miles" and "Back On The Chain Gang," to rarer gems like "The Phone Call," "Chill Factor" and "Criminal"—are treated to all-acoustic arrangements and backed by the acclaimed Duke Quartet, a classical ensemble that takes the quintessential rock 'n' roll of the Pretenders into a lush, elegant and resonant new realm. Ably assisting in this remarkable stylistic foray are producer Stephen Street, on hand for tracks from the group's 1994 release Last of The Independents, keyboardist Damon Albarn of the group Blur and percussionist Mark Smith.

The result is an album that emphatically underlines the songwriting art that has always been at the heart of the Pretenders' enduring appeal. Material that seemed to spring, fully-formed, from the electric exchange of bass-drums-guitar, suddenly takes on new dimensions and unexpected nuances in this acoustic setting; lyrics and melody emerge to make the most familiar song fresh again and the interplay between these gifted musicians has whole new territories in which to stretch and grow. Simply put, The Isle Of View, on Warner Bros. Records, is an ear-opening new take on one of the most influential groups in modern music.

The impetus for The Isle of View first emerged during sessions for the above mentioned Last Of The Independents, the triumphant return-to-form that marked the Pretenders' first consistent line-up since their formation. "We cut a version of 'Angel Of The Morning,' to use as a B-side," explains Chrissie Hynde, "and Stephen Street, who produced the track, suggested we use the Duke Quartet, whom he'd worked with in the past. I loved the results. The sound of the strings meshed with the band so well that the idea of working with that kind of instrumentation just stayed with me."

The Merrilee Rush/Juice Newton classic was, it turned out, just the beginning. After touring in support of Last Of The Independents, including select club dates and a turn through Spain, Chrissie and the group, sparked by the energy of the road, wanted to keep working. "We were really having fun," Chrissie explains, "and wanted to keep it going. That's when the idea of an acoustic album came up. Not only would we get the chance to keep playing, but it gave us an excuse to work with the Duke Quartet again."

It was in January of this year that Chrissie and Pretenders guitarist Adam Seymour began culling the group's extensive catalogue for material best suited to an unamplified approach.

Pretenders are:

Chrissie Hynde: vocals, guitar

Adam Seymour: guitar, vocals, harmonium

Martin Chambers: drums

Andy Hobson: bass guitar

"We originally had in mind to do more obscure tracks," Chrissie explains. "But, in the end, the criterion was what worked best for the instruments and that turned out to include some hits."

The process yielded interesting, and unexpected, results. Chrissie: "A song like 'I Hurt You,' was a natural for strings, while 'Chill Factor,' which was originally on our third album, was not an obvious choice, but worked very well in this context. It was great to strip back these songs to their bare essentials, to take away all the studio touches and refinements and hear them in their most basic form. I think that's a good test of any song, to see if it stands on its own."

Following rehearsals with the full band, "sitting around my living room in a circle," explains Chrissie, the next step was incorporating the Duke Quartet into the mix. "John Metcalfe, the quartet's viola player, worked with us in writing the arrangements," she continues. "There was a lot of interaction. We kind of elaborated on each other. The Pretenders are not the most experimental group around. In many ways we're very traditional. But we were very drawn to the acoustic idea and I think the music reflects that."

It does indeed. Recorded before a live audience in May at London's Jacob Street Studios, The Isle of View captures the Pretenders making up in the pure pleasure of performance what they've sacrificed in sheer volume. "Instead of sticks, Martin at one point was playing drums with two ball point pens," Chrissie reveals. "Everybody had fun, doing whatever it took to make the music work."

That fun, and the full impact of the music, have also been captured on a special longform video of the concert, to be released in conjunction with the audio version by Warner Video. At the same time, No Turn Left Unstoned, an hour-long documentary chronicling the tumultuous life and times of the Pretenders, and featuring interviews with everyone from Elvis Costello and Rosanna Arquette to the surviving members of the original line-up, is set to air on both sides of the Atlantic. Meanwhile, the song that started it all, "Angel Of The Morning," has turned up as a featured track on the just released soundtrack to the hit NBC-TV series Friends, where Chrissie herself made a recent guest appearance to perform the cut.

'I like to think of the Pretenders as a group somewhere in mid-career," says Chrissie of the outfit she has fronted for fifteen years and who recently graced the stage at the opening of the Rock 'N' Roll Hall Of Fame in her home state of Ohio. "We've got time to try all sorts of things. I don't think of this album as some kind of drastic departure. We'll always be a rock 'n' roll band. This is just a way of keeping things fresh."

Sense of Purpose

Everybody chokes
When they see someone cut down in their prime
It may not show when you look at me
But I know I'm in mine

I'm potent, baby I'm potent
Dangerous to the naked eye
Rest your head on this bed of mother's pride
And find out why

Don't you wanna take me home?
Don't you wanna take me home?

Give me a sense of purpose
A real sense of purpose now
Give me a sense of purpose
A real sense of purpose now

Bully boys don't bother me
I purse my lips and they run away
Guys like you who are gentle and true
Don't come around here every day

I'm potent, baby I'm potent
Just one swig of me would get most guys smashed
But a drop of yours makes me stagger and swerve
I guess I'm outclassed

Everybody chokes
When they see someone cut down in their prime
Take this plea to your heart
Lift me in mine

Don't you wanna take me home?
Don't you wanna take me home?

Baby!
Give me a sense of purpose
A real sense of purpose now

Let's get on outta here now
Let's go!

I Hurt You

I been crying like a woman
Cos I'm mad, mad, mad like a man
If you'd been in the S.S. in '43
You'd have been kicked out for cruelty

I hurt you
Cos you hurt me
So I hurt you
Cos you hurt me!

I've been wonderin', 'bout your dependency
Your idea of defiance is a modern-day mystery
Your arms and chest are cold when your back is on fire
And the only time that you come clean
Is when you're talking to your buyer

I hurt you
Cos you hurt me
So I hurt you
Cos you hurt me!

Forget our philosophies
That we admired when we were young
And our popular points of view
They can't mean much, or nothing, or something, or anything
If we can't say I love you

Happy birthday baby, thank you for the schooling
Your correction mistress warned me, man she wasn't fooling
Never trust a user with your television overnight
And don't try to paint your masterpeice under artificial light

I hurt you
Cos you hurt me
So I hurt you
Cos you hurt me!

Back on the Chain Gang

I found a picture of you, oh
What hijacked my world that night?
To a place in the past we've been cast out of, oh
Now we're back in the fight

We're back on the train, oh
Back on the chain gang

Circumstance beyond our control, oh
The phone, T.V. and the News Of The World
Got in the house like a pigeon from hell, oh
Threw sand in our eyes and descended like flies

Put us back on the train, oh
Back in the train gang

The powers that be
That force us to live like we do
Bring me to my knees
When I see what they've done to you
But I'll die as I stand here today
Knowing that deep in my heart
They'll fall to ruin one day
For making us part

I found a picture of you, oh
Those were the happiest days of my life
Like a break in the battle was your part, oh
In the wretched life of a lonely heart

Now we're back on the train, oh
Back on the chain gang

I Go to Sleep

When I look up from my pillow
I dream you are there with me
Though you are far away
I know you'll always be near to me

I go to sleep, sleep and imagine that you're there with me
I go to sleep, sleep and imagine that you're there with me

I look around me and
Feel you are ever so close to me
Each tear that flows from my eye
Brings back mem'ries of you to me

I go to sleep, sleep and imagine that you're there with me
I go to sleep, sleep and imagine that you're there with me

I was wrong, I will cry
I will love you till the day I die
You are all, you alone and no-one else
You were meant for me

When morning comes again
I have the loneliness you left me
Each day drags by until
Finally night time descends on me

I go to sleep, sleep and imagine that you're there with me
I go to sleep, sleep and imagine that you're there with me

Chill Factor

She's getting older
Yeah, she's getting wise
But a change has changed the girl
Gone's the sparkle from her eyes
She wants to be a good mother
So she'll do the best she can
But what about the other
What about the man

Well it's cold to leave a woman
With family on her own
It's chill factor
To the bone

She had her dreams too
But how can she pursue
Her ambitions
Be they great or small
You took her wings and flew
But remember when you're through
Your rise was due
To somebody else's fall

When the hard part's over
And the kids've almost grown
You'll be their big hero
Whenever you make it home
Shower them with presents
Things she could never buy
Delight them with your stories
About the great big
The great big world outside
But dig

It's cold to leave a woman
With family on her own
It's chill factor, chill factor
Chill factor to the bone

Resignation in her sighs
Is a sorry indication
Of how time
Can brutalise
Take away the hope
And the will will follow
Take away the faith
And goodbye tomorrow

It's cold to leave a woman
With family on her own
It's chill factor
To the bone

2000 Miles

He's gone
2000 miles
Is very far
The snow is falling down
Gets colder day by day
I miss you
The children will sing
He'll be back at Christmas time

In these frozen and silent nights
Sometimes in a dream
You appear
Outside under the purple sky
Diamonds in the snow
Sparkle
Our hearts were singing
It felt like Christmas time

2000 miles
Is very far through the snow
I'll think of you
Wherever you go

He's gone
2000 miles
Is very far
The snow is falling down
Gets colder day by day
I miss you
I hear people singing
It must be Christmas time

I can hear people singing
It must be Christmas time

The Phone Call

This is a mercy mission
From a faceless messenger who don't wanna see you hit
Here's the word, listen to it
Somebody that you used to know is back in town
You better go

This is a mercy mission
A voice you'll never hear again from a southside callbox
Winged demons are the hardest to outfox
The same one you lost on the run
Gonna show you that it ain't no fun

You better get out of town
Cos you're gonna get hit
I didn't wanna see you hit

This is a mercy mission
You'll find your schedule underneath the door
All the arrangements have been made
Major expenses have been paid (as you know)
Don't forget the last detail
Accept no parcels in the mail

Criminal

Look at me
High upon the hill
You could say
I'm on top of the world
Baby, I'm blue
All because of you

I can see this city
Crumble all around me
Press me to your chest
Block out the view
Oh, whoa, whoa, whoa

You made me
Some kind of criminal
You put me outlaw
Because I loved you

The first thing I think when I wake up
When can I see you?
The last thing I think when I'm drifting off
When will I see you?

Oh, look at me
I'm addicted still
At first I refused
Now I just swallow the pill
Oh, baby, won't you
Fix me like you used to?

I could spend my time in hell
I might as well
Cos hell is where I'm bound to dwell
Without you
Oh, whoa, whoa, whoa

You made me
Some kind of criminal
You put me outlaw
Because I loved you, yeah

In my time
One thing I've learned
If you play with fire
You get burned, oh
Baby, it's true
I got burned by you

I put everything I had
Into a bag
And trusted you to do
What you didn't do
Oh, whoa, whoa, whoa

You made me
Some kind of criminal
You put me outlaw
Because I loved you, yeah

Private Life

Your private life drama baby leave me out
Your private life drama baby leave me out

J'ai les glands with your theatrics
Your acting's a drag
It's O.K. on T.V. cos you can turn it off
But don't try me
Yes your marriage is a tragedy
But it's not my concern
I'm very superficial, I hate anything official

Your private life drama baby leave me out
You've been lying to someone and now me - Stop!
Your private life drama baby leave me out
You've been lying to someone and now me - Stop!
Your private life drama baby leave me out
You've been lying to someone and now me - Stop!
Your private life drama baby leave me
You've been lying to someone and now me

Sentimental gestures only bore me to death
You've made a desperate appeal
Now save your breath
Attachment to obligation
Through guilt and regret shit that's so wet
And your sex-life complications
Are not my fascinations

Your private life drama baby leave me out
You've been lying to someone and now me - Stop!
Your private life drama baby leave me out
You've been lying to someone and now me - Stop!
Your private life drama baby leave me out
You've been lying to someone and now me - Stop!
Your private life drama baby leave me out
You've been lying to someone and now me

You asked me for advice, I said 'use the door'
But you're still clinging to somebody you deplore
And now you wanna use me for emotional blackmail
I just feel pity when you lie, contempt when you cry

Your Private life drama baby leave me out
You've been lying to someone and now me - Stop!
Private life drama baby leave me out
You've been lying to someone and now me - Stop!
Your private life, private life leave me out
You've been lying to someone and now me - Stop!
Private life drama baby leave me out
You've been lying to someone and now me

Hymn to Her

Let me inside you, into your room
I've heard it's lined with the things you don't show
Lay me beside you down on the floor
I've been your lover from the womb to the tomb
I dress as your daughter when the moon becomes round
You be my mother when everything's gone

And she will always carry on
Something is lost, but something is found
They will keep on speaking her name
Somethings change, some stay the same

Keep beckoning to me from behind that closed door
The maid and the mother and the crone that's grown old
I hear your voice coming out of that hole
I listen to you and I want some more
I listen to you and I want some more

And she will always carry on
Something is lost, but something is found
They will keep on speaking her name
Somethings change, some stay the same

Let me inside you, into your room
I've heard it's lined with the things you don't show
Lay me beside you, down on the floor
I've been your lover from the womb to the tomb
I dress as your daughter when the moon becomes round
You be my mother when everything's gone

And she will always carry on
Something is lost, but something is found
They will keep on speaking her name
Somethings change, some stay the same

Kid

Kid, what changed your mood
You've gone all sad so I feel sad too
I think I know
Some things you never outgrow
You think it's wrong
I can tell you do
How can I explain
You don't want me to

Kid, my only kid
You look so small, you've gone so quiet
I know you know what I'm about
I won't deny it
But you forgive
Though you don't understand
You've turned your head
You've dropped my hand

All my sorrow, all my blues
All my sorrow

Shut the light, go away
Full of grace, you cover your face

Kid, gracious kid
Your eyes are blue but you won't cry
I know angry tears are too dear
You won't let them go

Brass in Pocket

Got brass in pocket
Got bottle, I'm gonna use it
Intention, I feel inventive
Gonna make you, make you, make you notice

Got motion, restrained emotion
Been driving, Detroit leaning
No reason, just seems so pleasing
Gonna make you, make you, make you notice

Gonna use my arms, gonna use my legs
Gonna use my style gonna use my side step
Gonna use my fingers gonna use my, my, my imagination

Cos I gonna make you see
There's nobody else here no-one like me
I'm special, so special
I gotta have some of your attention, give it to me

Got rhythm, can't miss a beat
I got new skank, it's so reet
Got something I'm winking at you
Gonna make you, make you, make you notice

Gonna use my arms, gonna use my legs
Gonna use my style gonna use my side step
Gonna use my fingers gonna use my, my, my imagination

Cos I gonna make you see
There's nobody else here no-one like me
I'm special, so special
I gotta have some of your attention, give it to me

Oh, and when you walk . . .

Lovers of Today

I tried to talk to my baby
I said no, no, no, no, baby
Please don't cry
No, no, no, no, baby please
Cos all of the leaves come down
Everytime babies cry
All of the leaves come down

I put my arms round baby
I said hush, hush, hush
Hush baby sleep tight now
Hush, hush, hush, hush
Baby sleep
Cos all of the birds start to sing
Every time babies dream
All of the birds start to sing

Nobody wants to see
Lovers of today happy
So assume they're going to part
Nobody wants to be with
Someone so afraid
They'll be left with a broken heart

I kissed the eyes of my baby
I said dream, dream, dream
Baby all night long
Dream, dream all the night
Cos all of the stars in the skies
Twinkle in baby's eyes
All of the stars in the skies
Whoa, whoa, whoa

No, I'll never feel
Like a man in a man's world

Revolution

When we watch the children play
Remember
When it was me and you
So far away
The things we got up to
The funfair of danger
That's what set us apart
Couldn't wait for the real world
To test the strength
Of the lions heart

Cats like me and you
Have got laws
That they adhere to
Laws outside the laws
As laid down
By those we don't subscribe to
The world is getting stranger
But we'll never lose heart
We can't just wait for
The old guard to die
Before we can make a new start

Bring on the revolution
Keep the pressure on
I wanna die for something
Bring on the revolution
I wanna die for something
Wanna die for something
Bring on the revolution
I don't wanna die for nothing
Bring on the revolution
I wanna die for something, something

For every freedom fighter
I wanna hold on tighter
To the hope and will you gave
You were the brave
You were the brave
And one day
When I hear your children sing
Freedom will ring
Freedom!

When we watch the children play
Remember
How the priv'leged classes grew
And from this day
We set out to undo what won't undo
Looking for the grand in the minute
Every breath justifies
Every step that we take
To remove what the powers that be
Can't prove
And the children will understand why

Bring on the revolution
Keep the pressure on
I wanna die for something
Bring on the revolution
I wanna die for something
Wanna die for something
Bring on the revolution
I don't wanna die for nothing
Bring on the revolution
I wanna die for something, something

SENSE OF PURPOSE

Words and Music by
CHRISSIE HYNDE

© 1990 EMI MUSIC PUBLISHING LTD. trading as CLIVE BANKS SONGS
All Rights Controlled and Administered by EMI APRIL MUSIC INC.
All Rights Reserved   International Copyright Secured   Used by Permission

16

CHILL FACTOR

Words and Music by
CHRISSIE HYNDE

© 1986 EMI MUSIC PUBLISHING LTD. trading as CLIVE BANKS SONGS
All Rights Controlled and Administered by EMI APRIL MUSIC INC.
All Rights Reserved   International Copyright Secured   Used by Permission

PRIVATE LIFE

Words and Music by
CHRISSIE HYNDE

Pri-vate life dra-ma ba-by leave me out, pri-vate life dra-ma ba-by leave me.

Jai les glands with your the-a-trics, your act-ing's a drag,
Sen-ti-men-tal ges-tures on-ly bore me to death,
You asked me for ad-vice, I said, "Use the door,"

© 1980 EMI MUSIC PUBLISHING LTD. trading as CLIVE BANKS SONGS
All Rights Controlled and Administered by EMI APRIL MUSIC INC.
All Rights Reserved International Copyright Secured Used by Permission

BACK ON THE CHAIN GANG

Words and Music by
CHRISSIE HYNDE

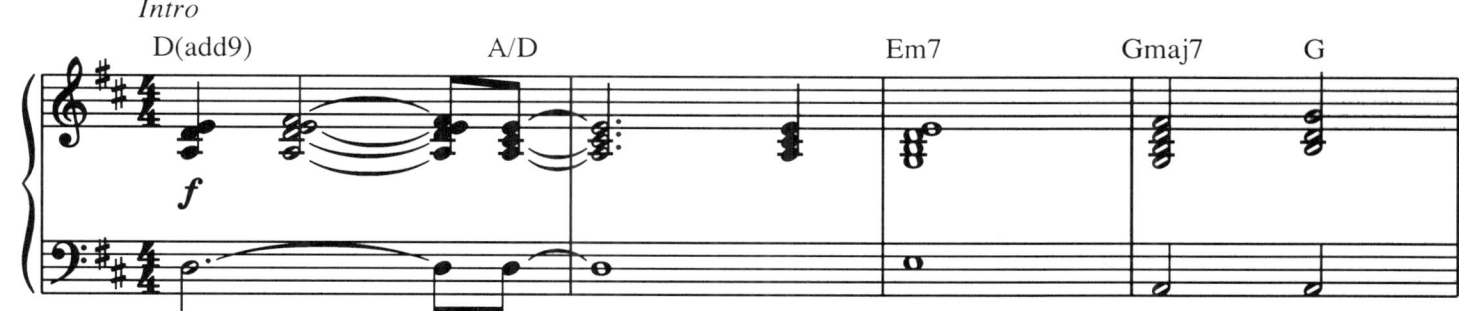
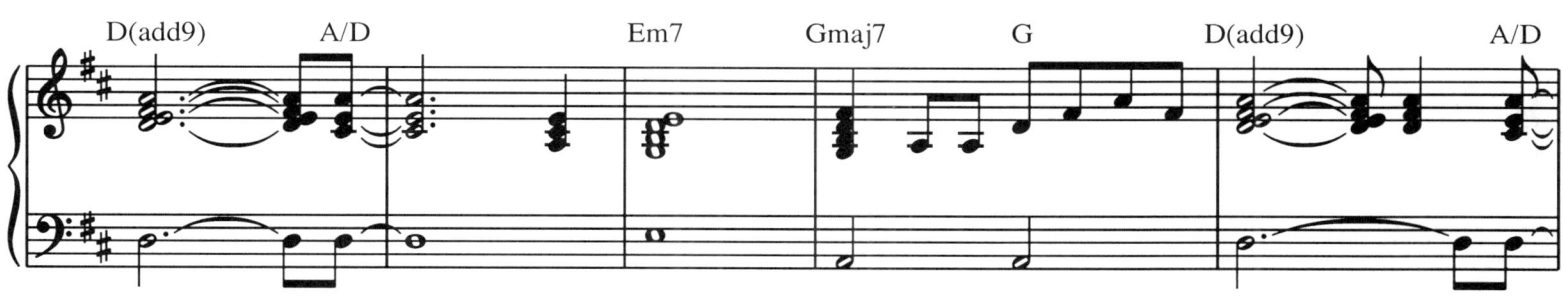

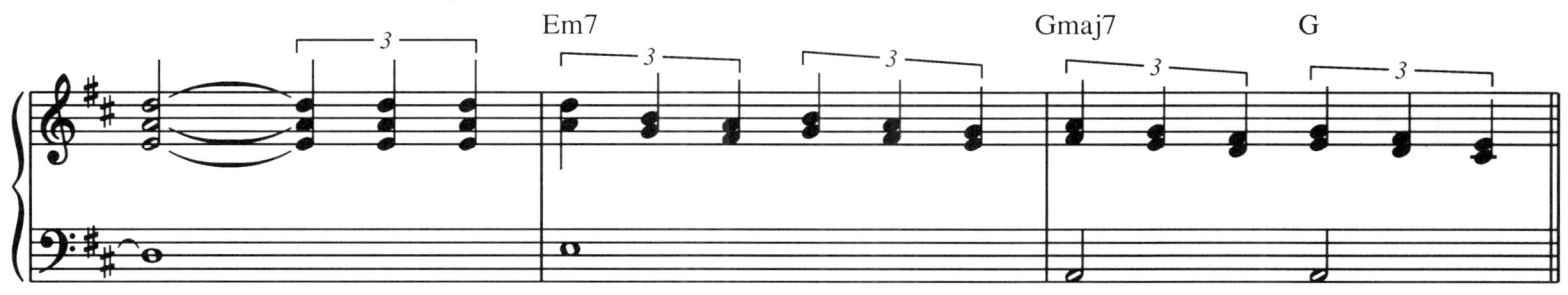

© 1982 EMI MUSIC PUBLISHING LTD. trading as CLIVE BANKS SONGS
All Rights Controlled and Administered by EMI APRIL MUSIC INC.
All Rights Reserved   International Copyright Secured   Used by Permission

28

KID

Words and Music by
CHRISSIE HYNDE

Moderately slow

Intro

Verse

Kid _____ what changed your mood, you've
Kid _____ my on - ly kid you

gone all _____ sad _____ so I feel _____ sad _____ too. I _____ think _____ I _____
look so _____ small, you've gone so _____ qui - et. I _____ know _____ you _____

_____ know, _____ some - things you nev - er out - grow. _____
_____ know _____ what I'm a - bout, I won't de - ny _____ it. _____

© 1979 EMI MUSIC PUBLISHING LTD. trading as CLIVE BANKS SONGS
All Rights Controlled and Administered by EMI APRIL MUSIC INC.
All Rights Reserved   International Copyright Secured   Used by Permission

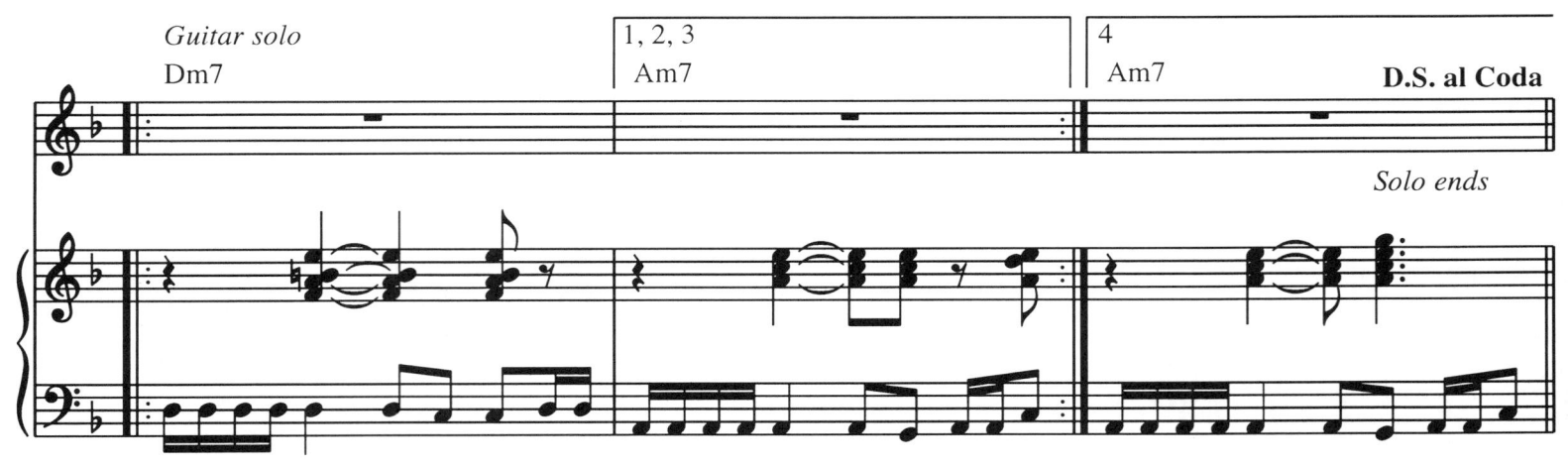

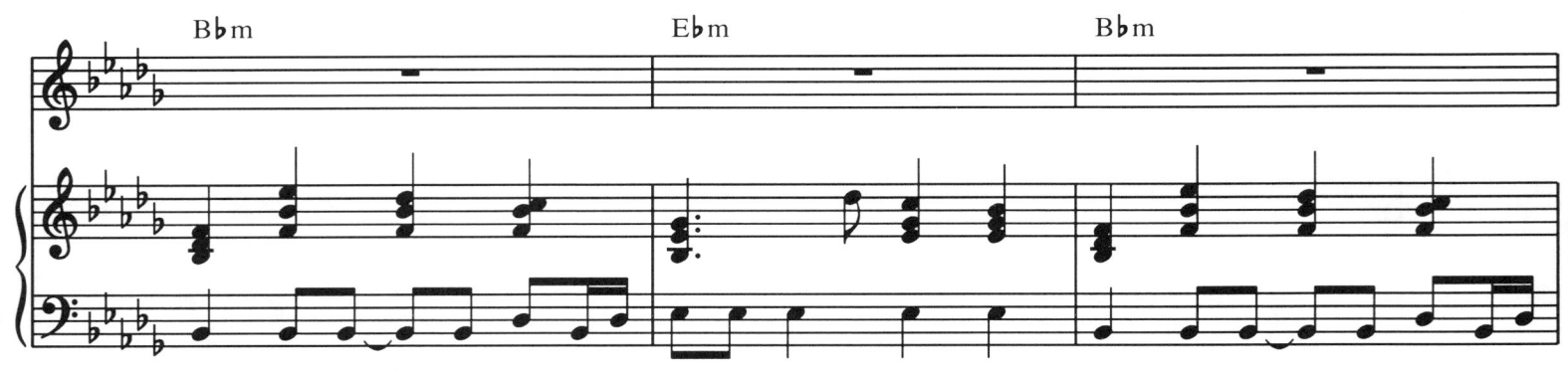
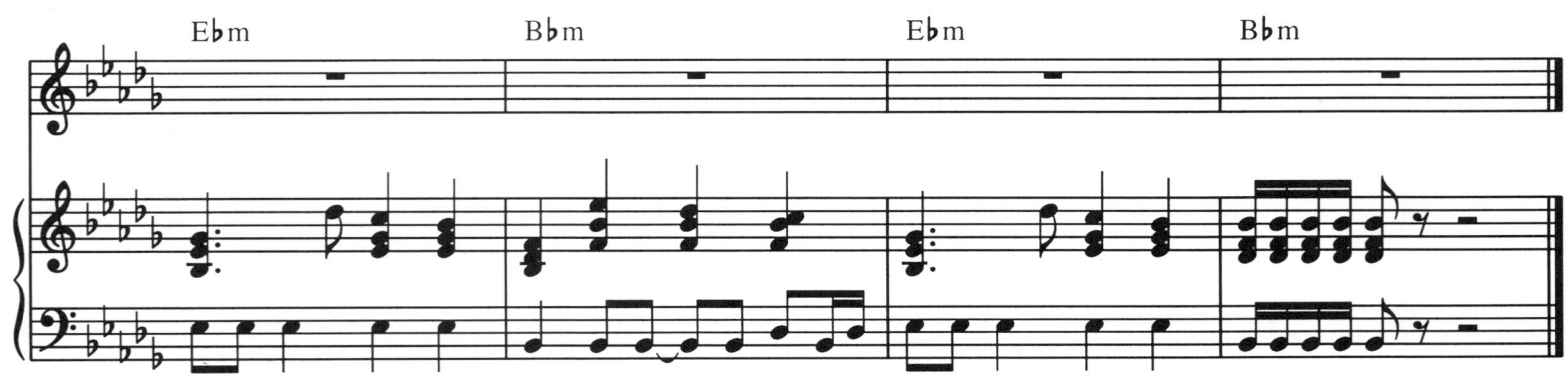

CRITICAL

BRASS IN POCKET

Words and Music by CHRISSIE HYNDE
and JAMES HONEYMAN-SCOTT

© 1979 EMI MUSIC PUBLISHING LTD. trading as CLIVE BANKS SONGS and JAMES HONEYMAN-SCOTT
All Rights for EMI MUSIC PUBLISHING LTD. trading as CLIVE BANKS SONGS Controlled and Administered by EMI APRIL MUSIC INC.
All Rights Reserved   International Copyright Secured   Used by Permission

2000 MILES

Words and Music by
CHRISSIE HYNDE

HYMN TO HER

Words and Music by
MEG KEENE

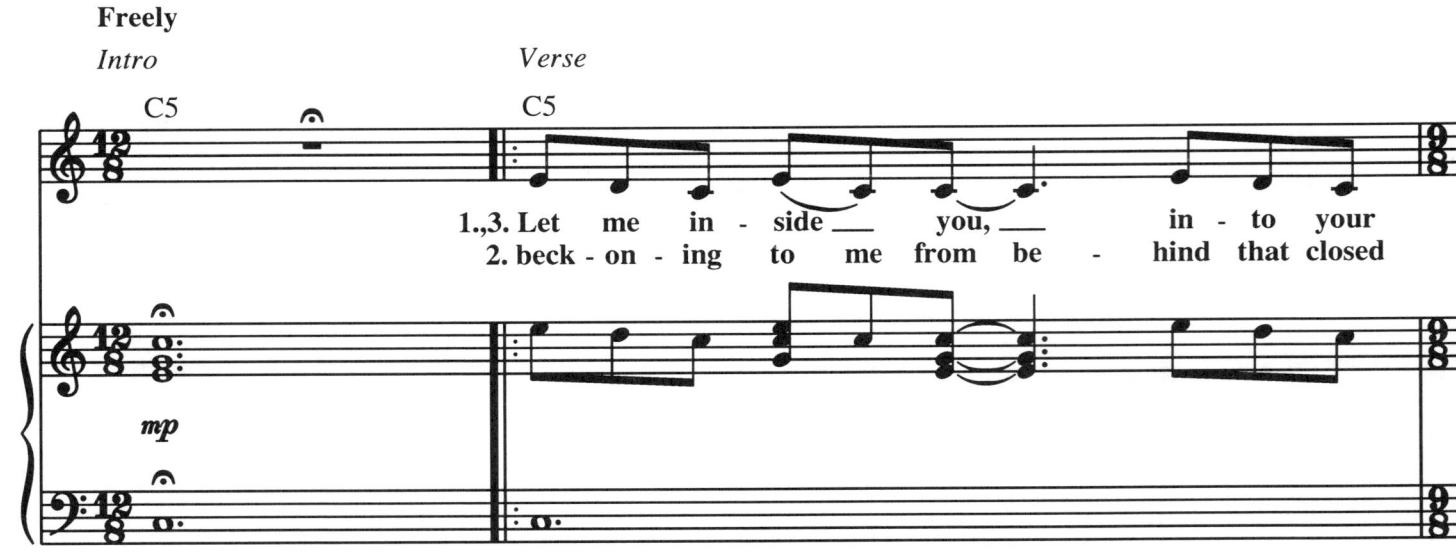

© 1986 HYNDE HOUSE OF HITS
All Rights Controlled and Administered by EMI APRIL MUSIC INC. under license from SONY/ATV TUNES LLC
All Rights Reserved   International Copyright Secured   Used by Permission

THE PHONE CALL

Words and Music by
CHRISSIE HYNDE

I GO TO SLEEP

Words and Music by
RAY DAVIES

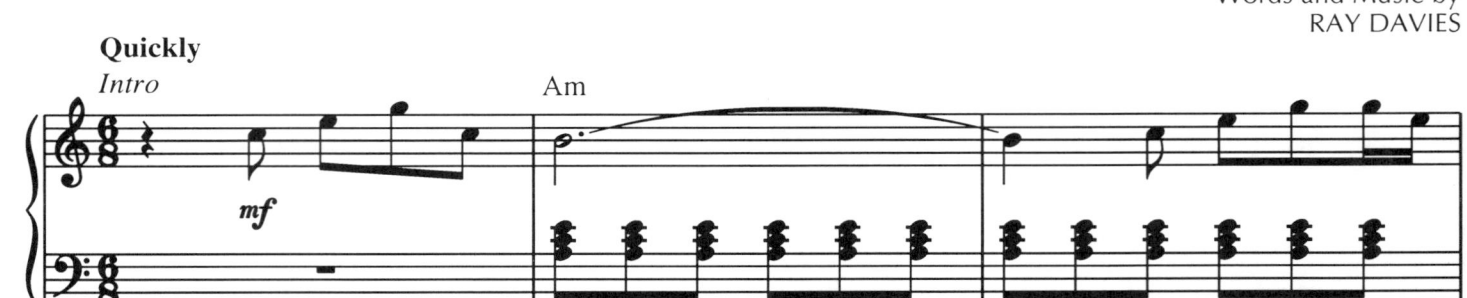

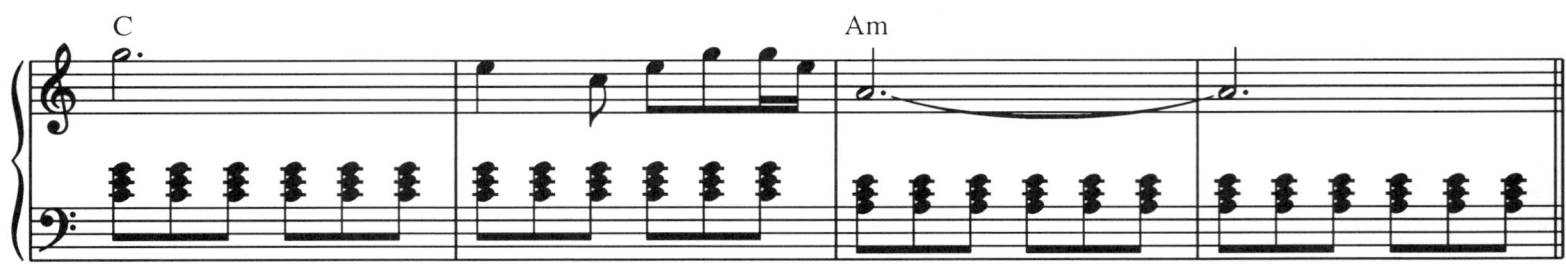

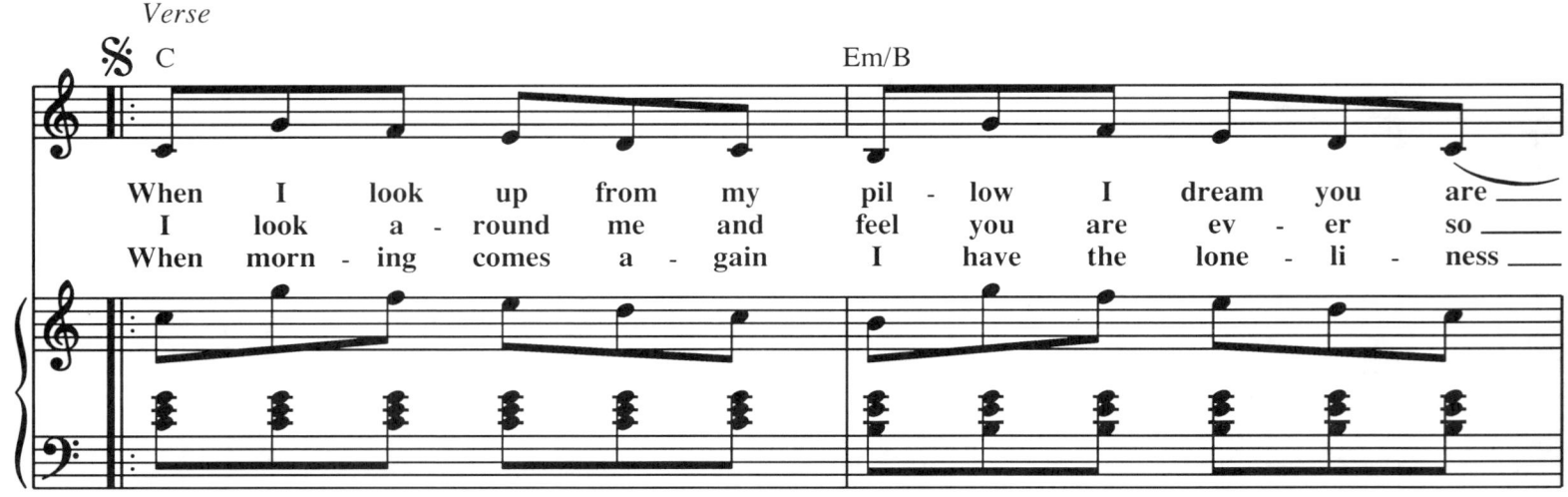

When I look up from my pil-low I dream you are there with me.
I look a-round me and feel you are ev-er so close to me.
When morn-ing comes a-gain I have the lone-li-ness you left me.

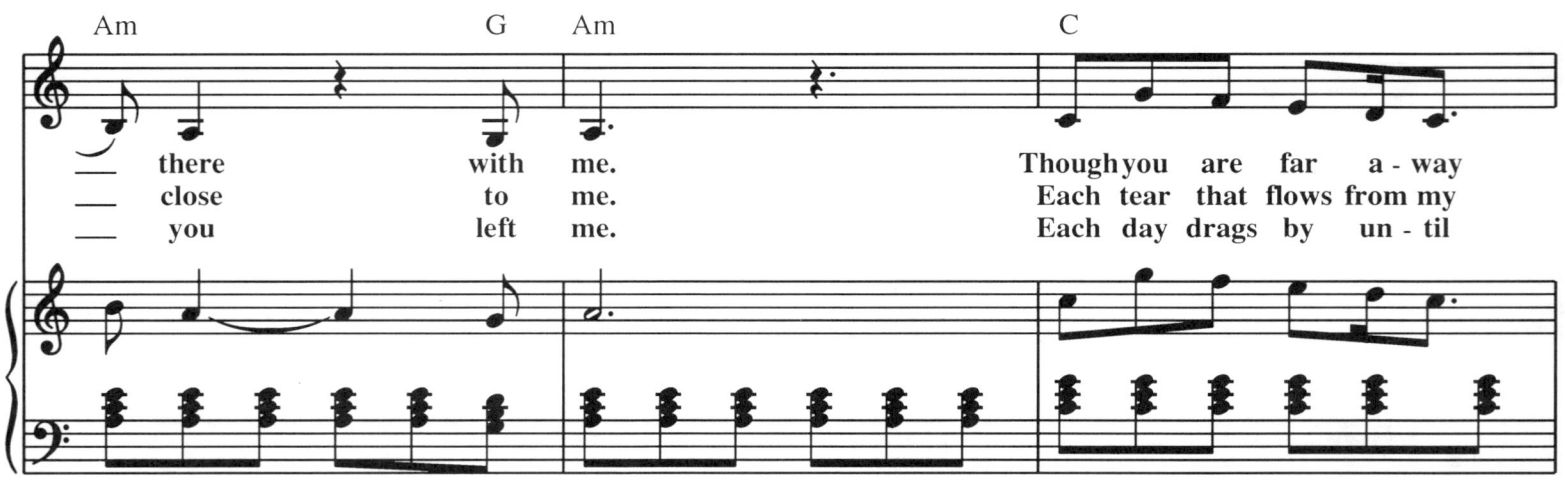

Though you are far a-way
Each tear that flows from my
Each day drags by un-til

Copyright © 1965 Edward Kassner Music Co., Ltd., for the World
Copyright Renewed
Controlled in the U.S.A. and Canada by Jay Boy Music Corp.
International Copyright Secured   All Rights Reserved

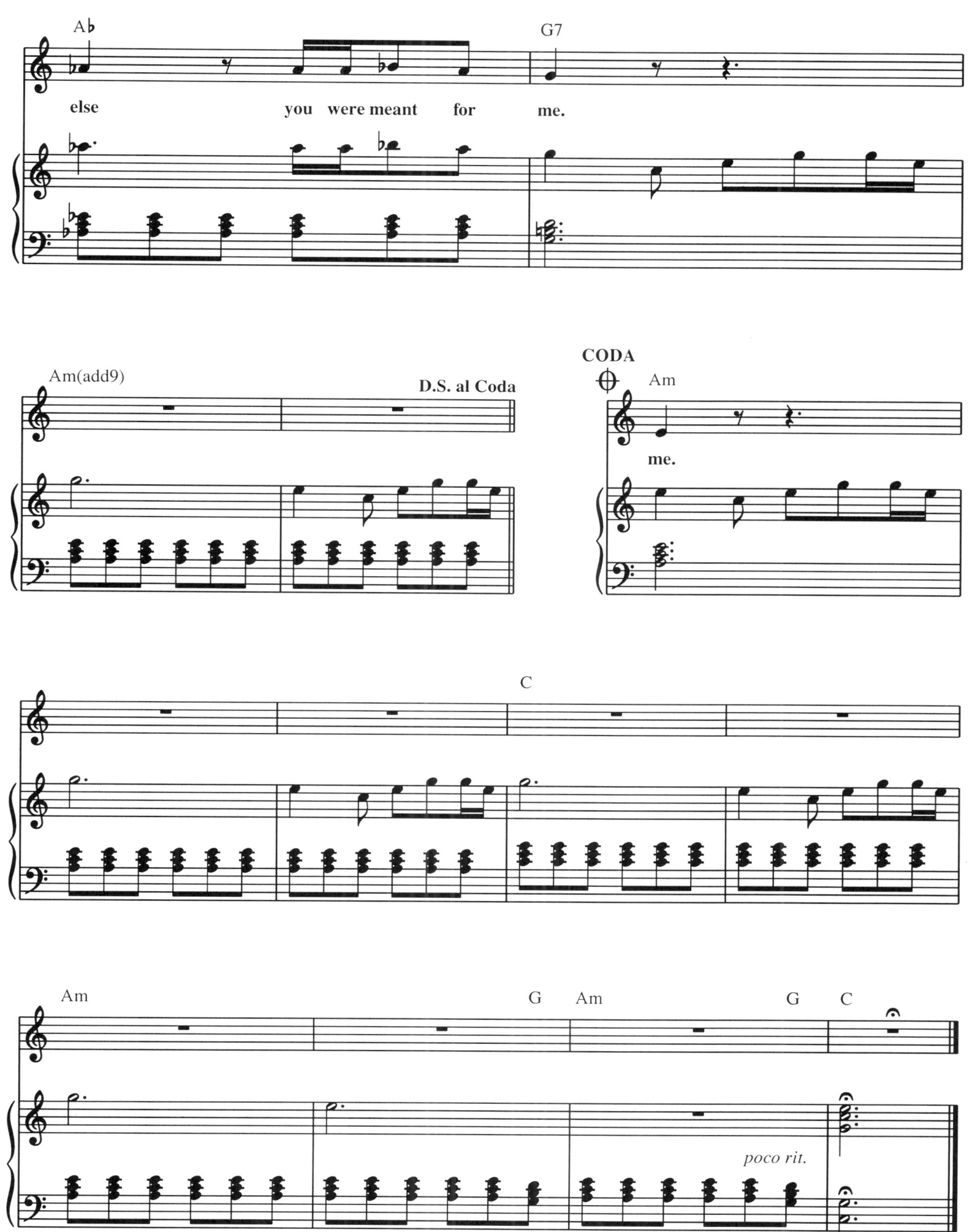

REVOLUTION

Words and Music by
CHRISSIE HYNDE

Moderate Rock

PRETENDERS
The Isle Of View

GUITAR PARTS

Sense of Purpose   88
Chill Factor   91
Private Life   94
Back On The Chain Gang   99
Kid   102
I Hurt You   105
Criminal   109
Brass In Pocket   113
2000 Miles   114
Hymn To Her   116
Lovers Of Today   117
The Phone Call   121
I Go To Sleep   116
Revolution   124

SENSE OF PURPOSE
(Guitar Part)

Words and Music by
CHRISSIE HYNDE

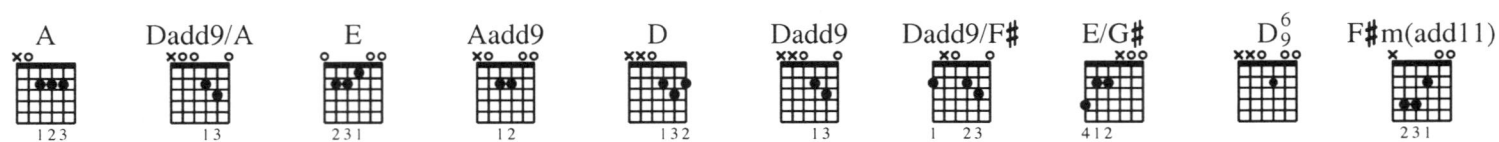

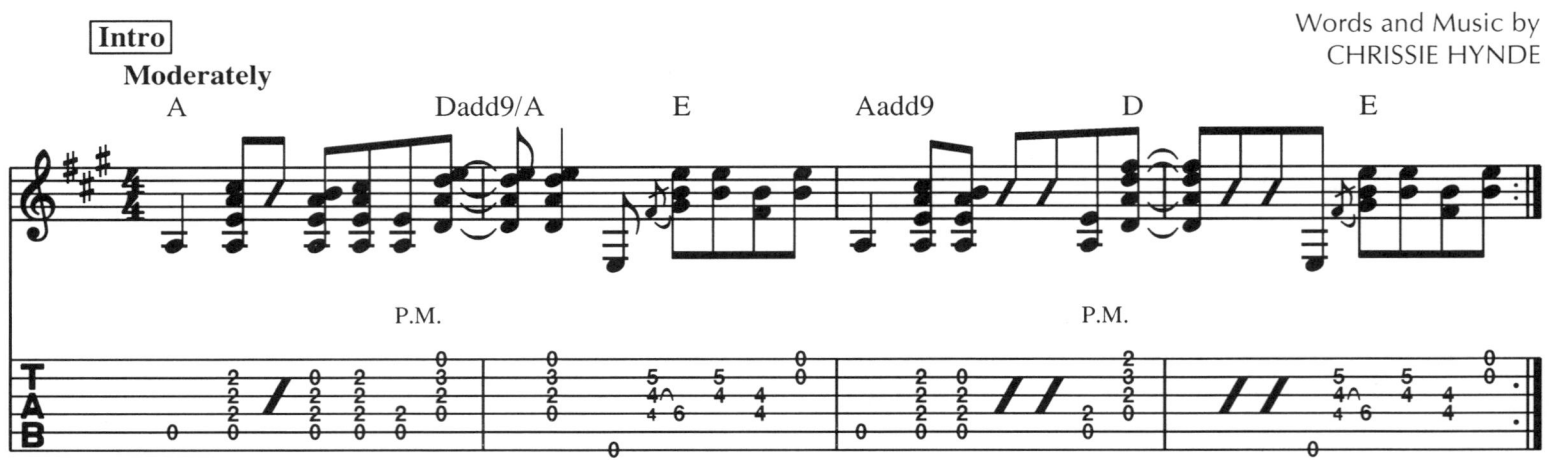

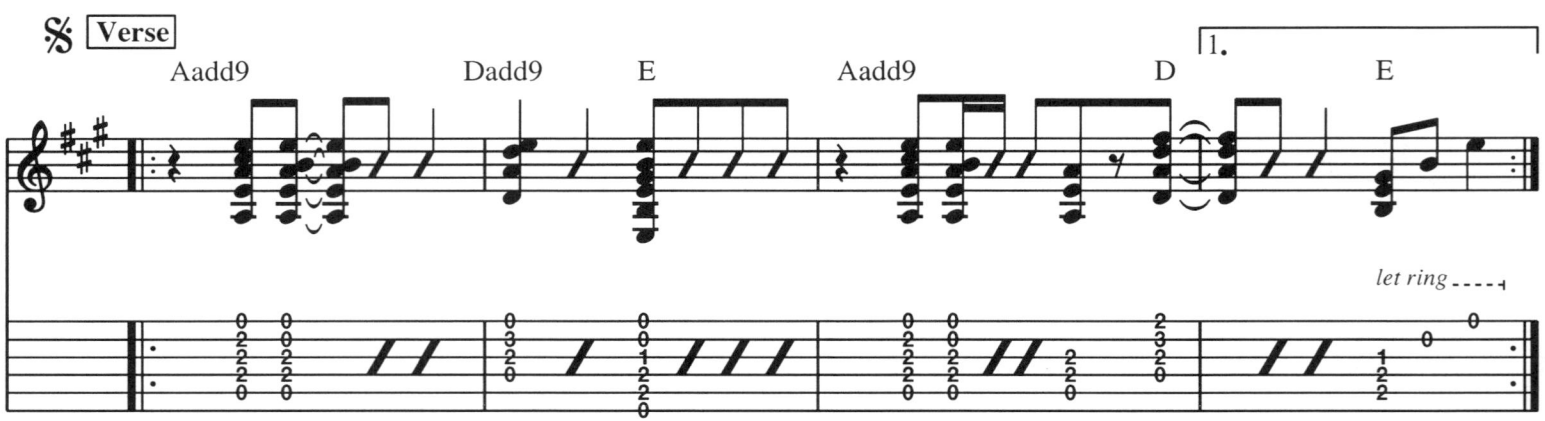

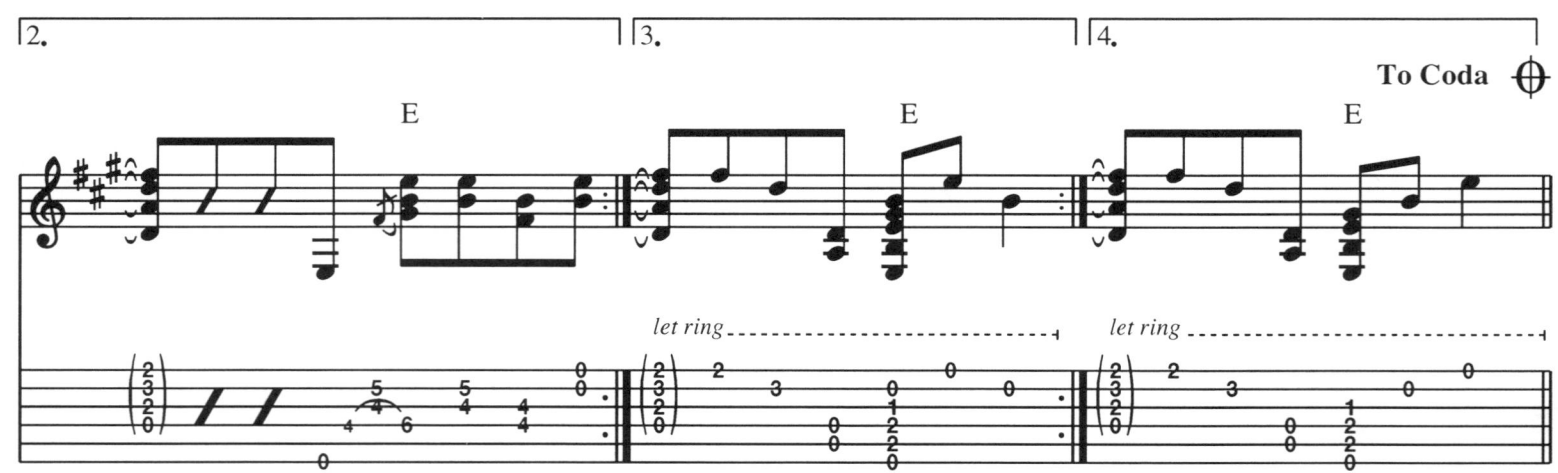

© 1990 EMI MUSIC PUBLISHING LTD, trading as CLIVE BANKS SONGS
All Rights Controlled and Administered by EMI APRIL MUSIC INC.
All Rights Reserved   International Copyright Secured   Used by Permission

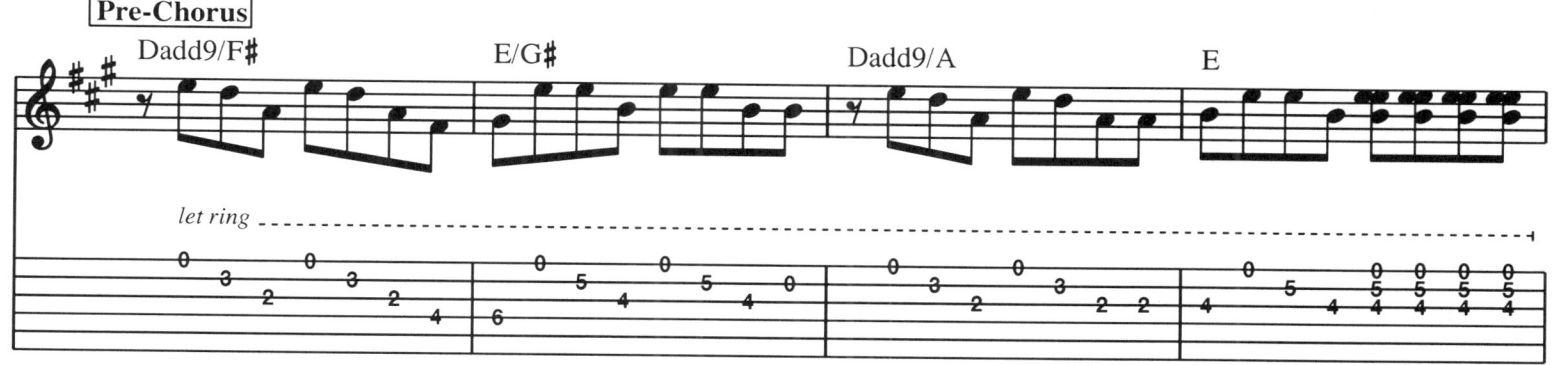
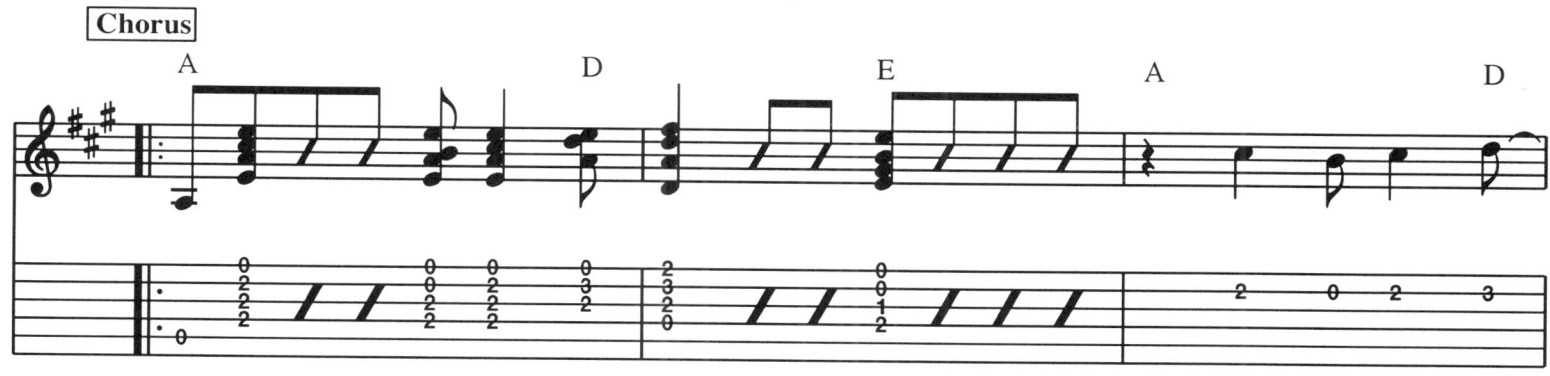
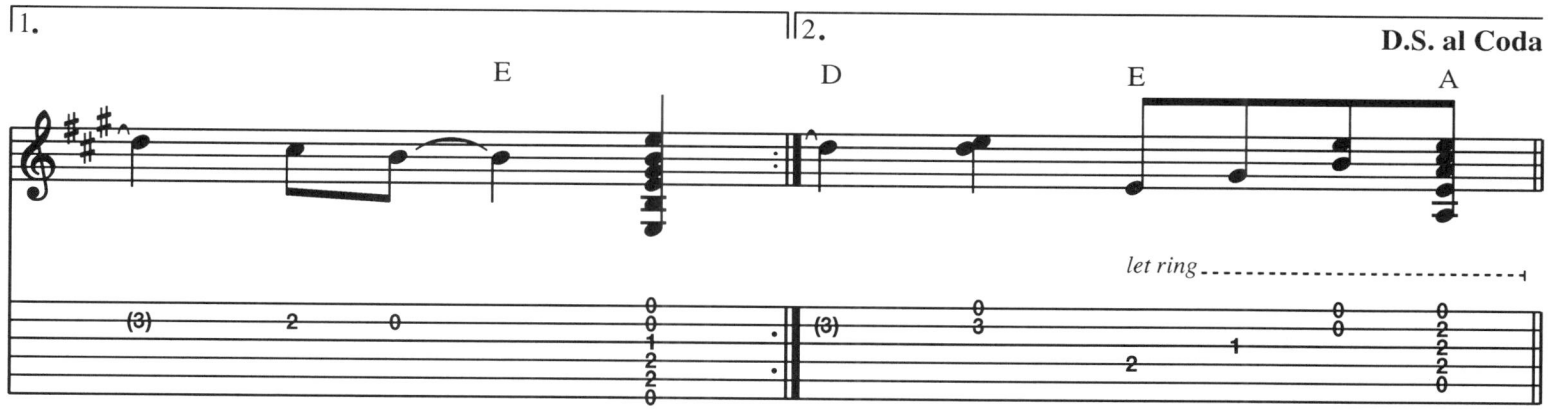
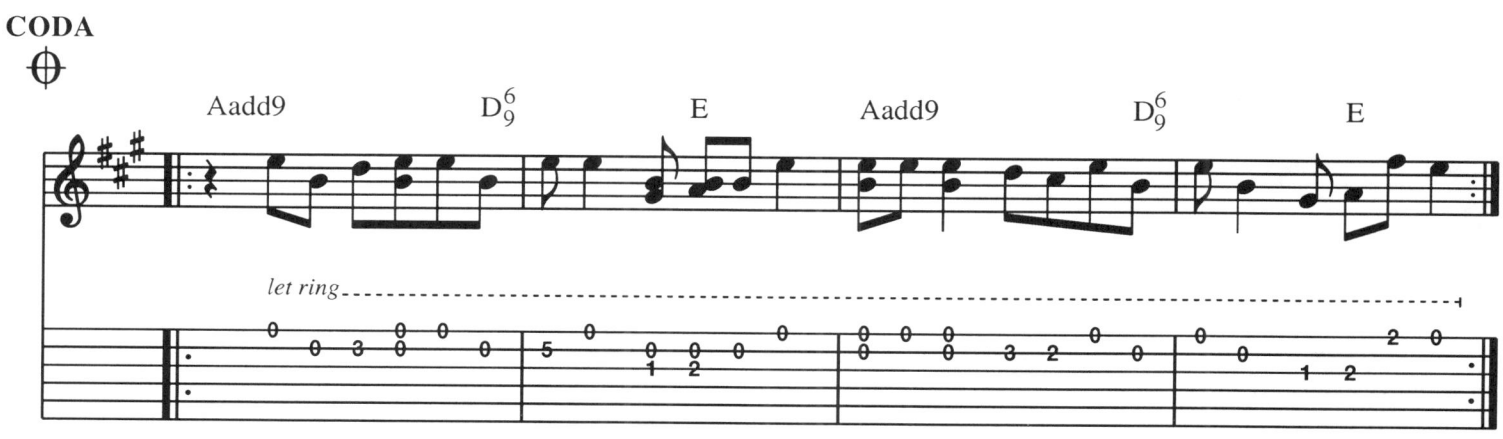

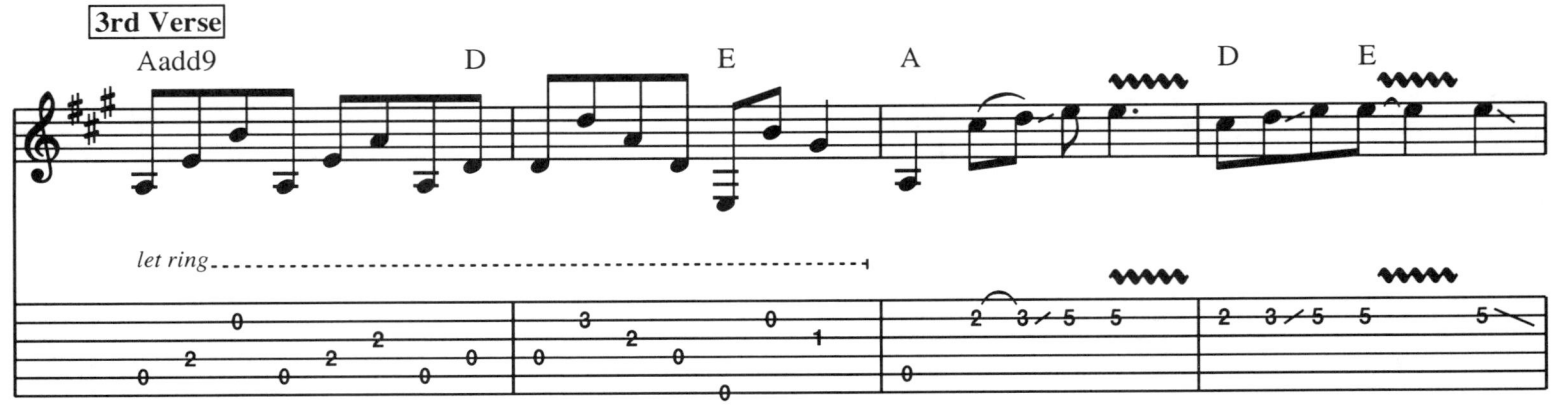
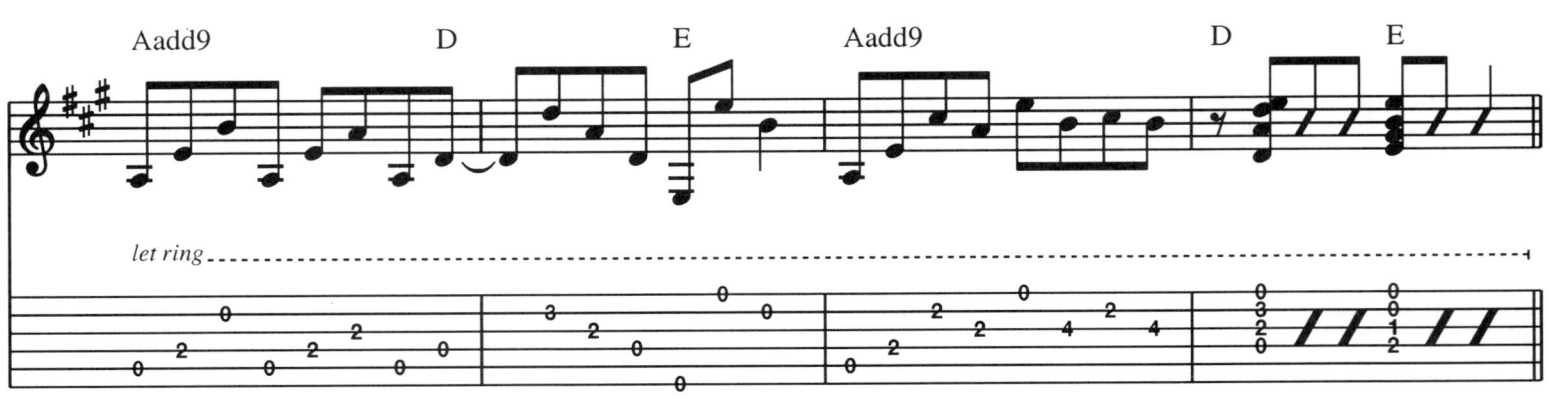
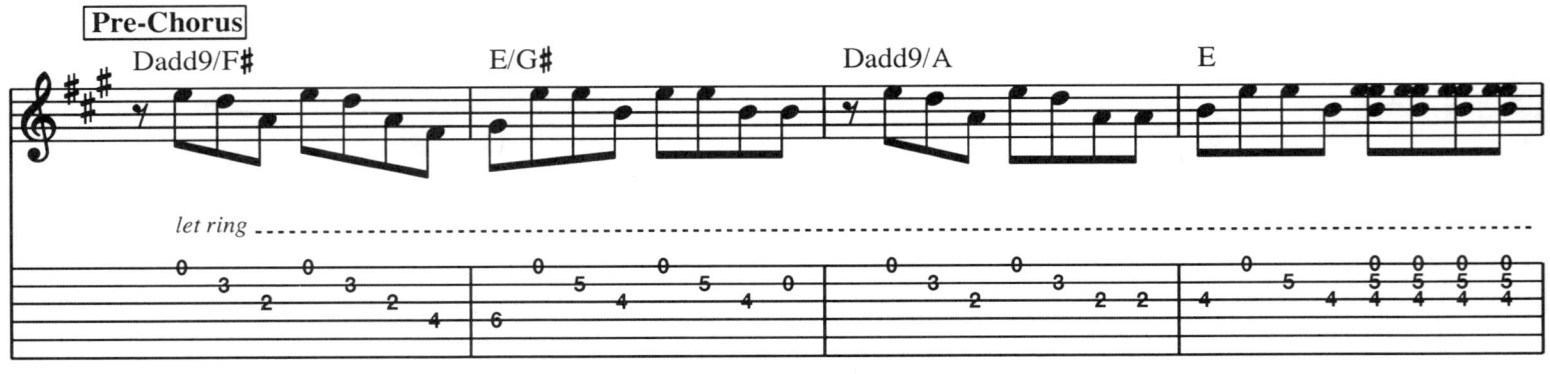
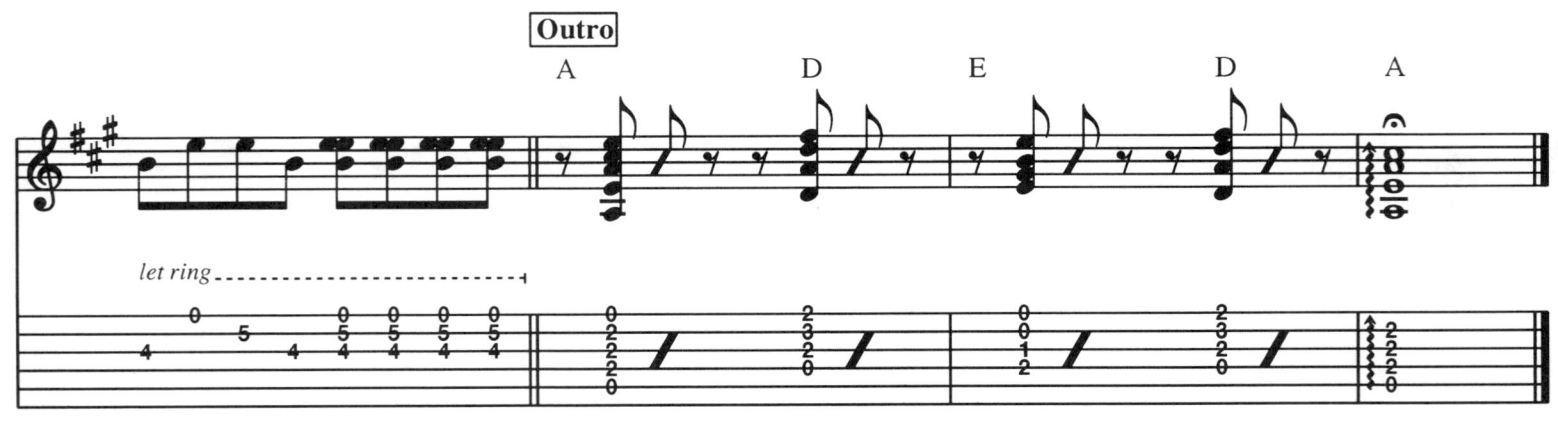

CHILL FACTOR
(Guitar Part)

Words and Music by
CHRISSIE HYNDE

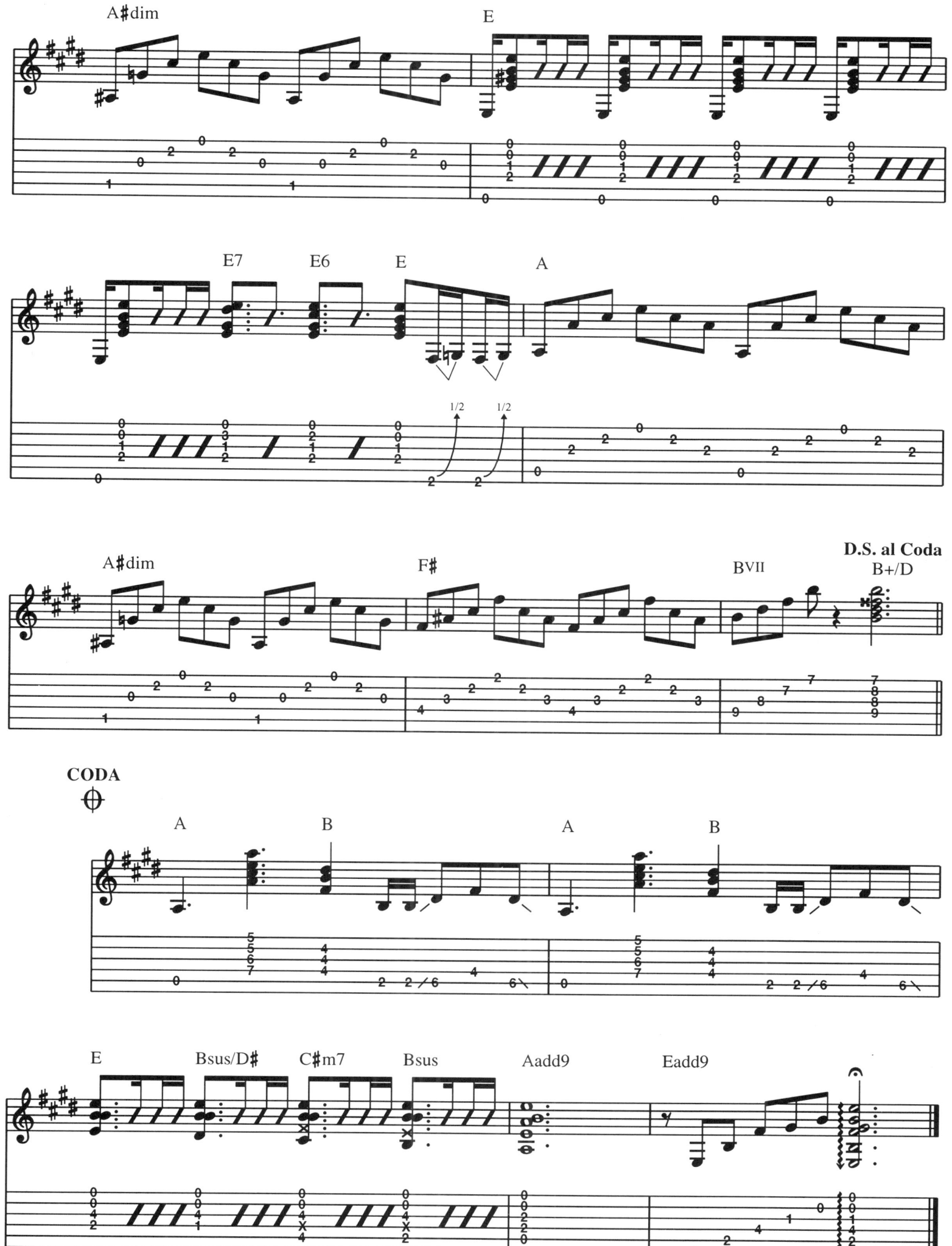

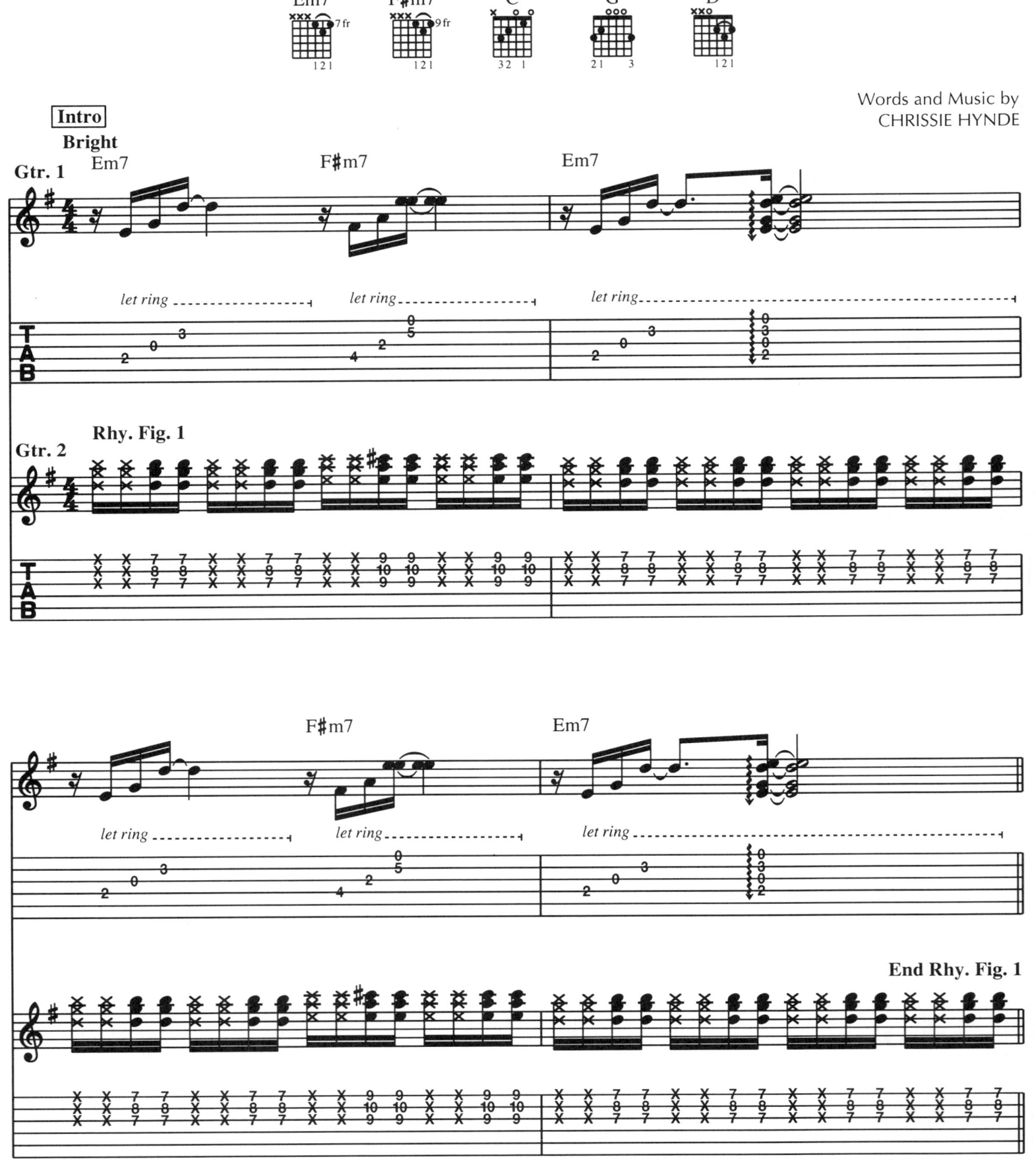

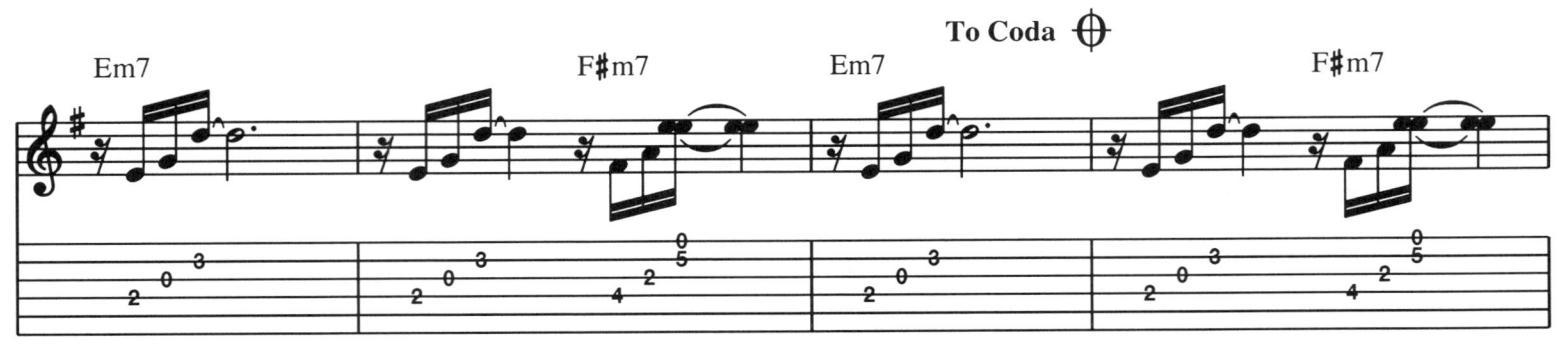
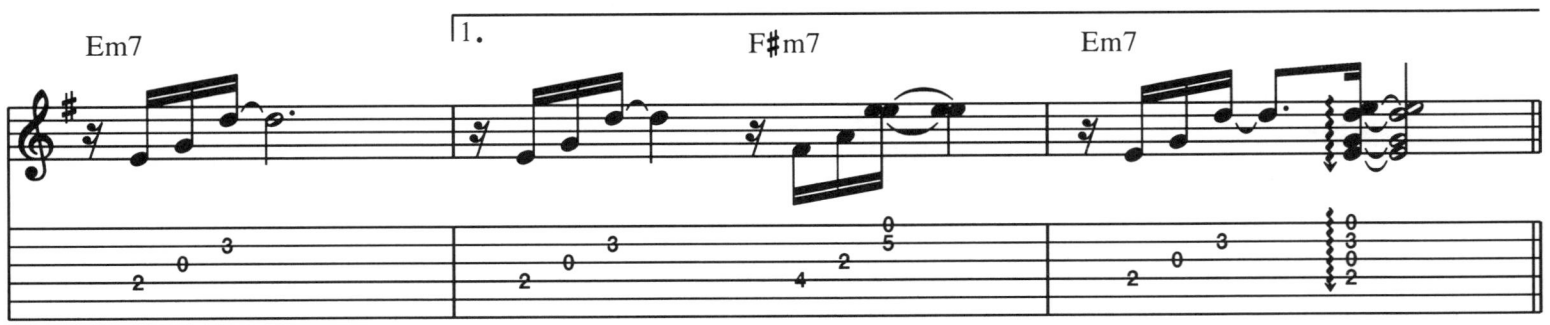

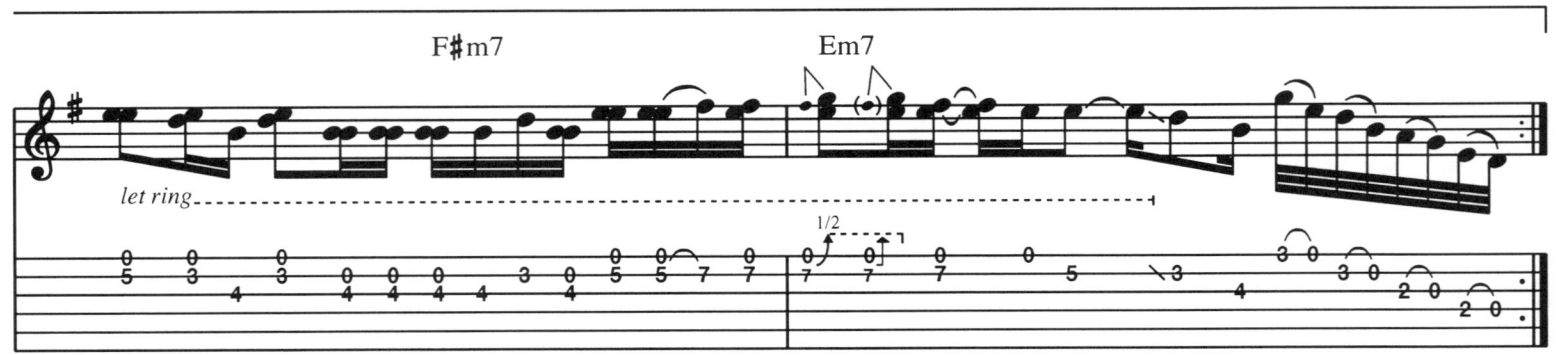
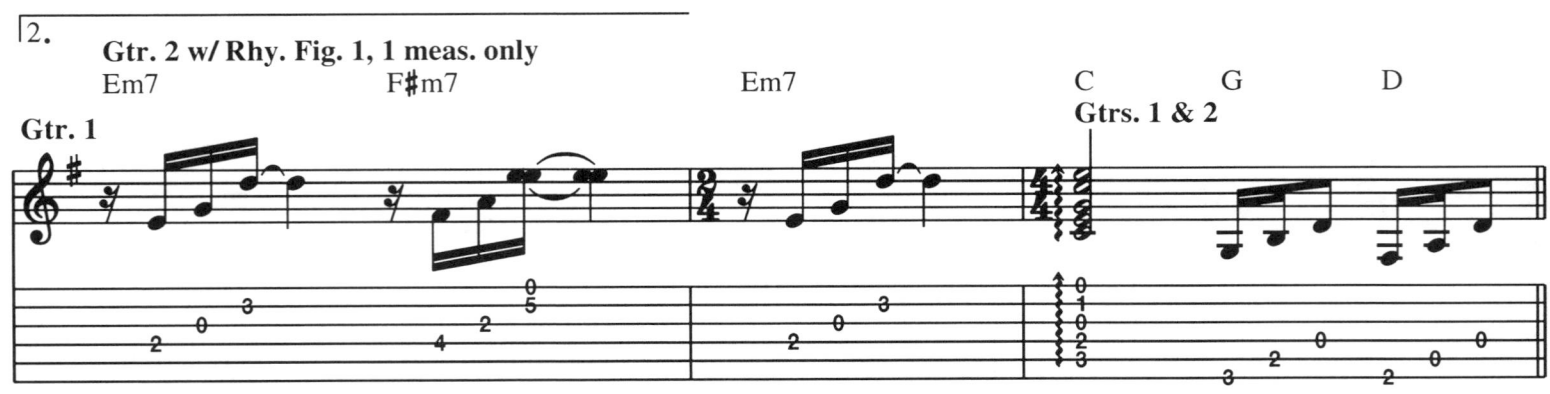

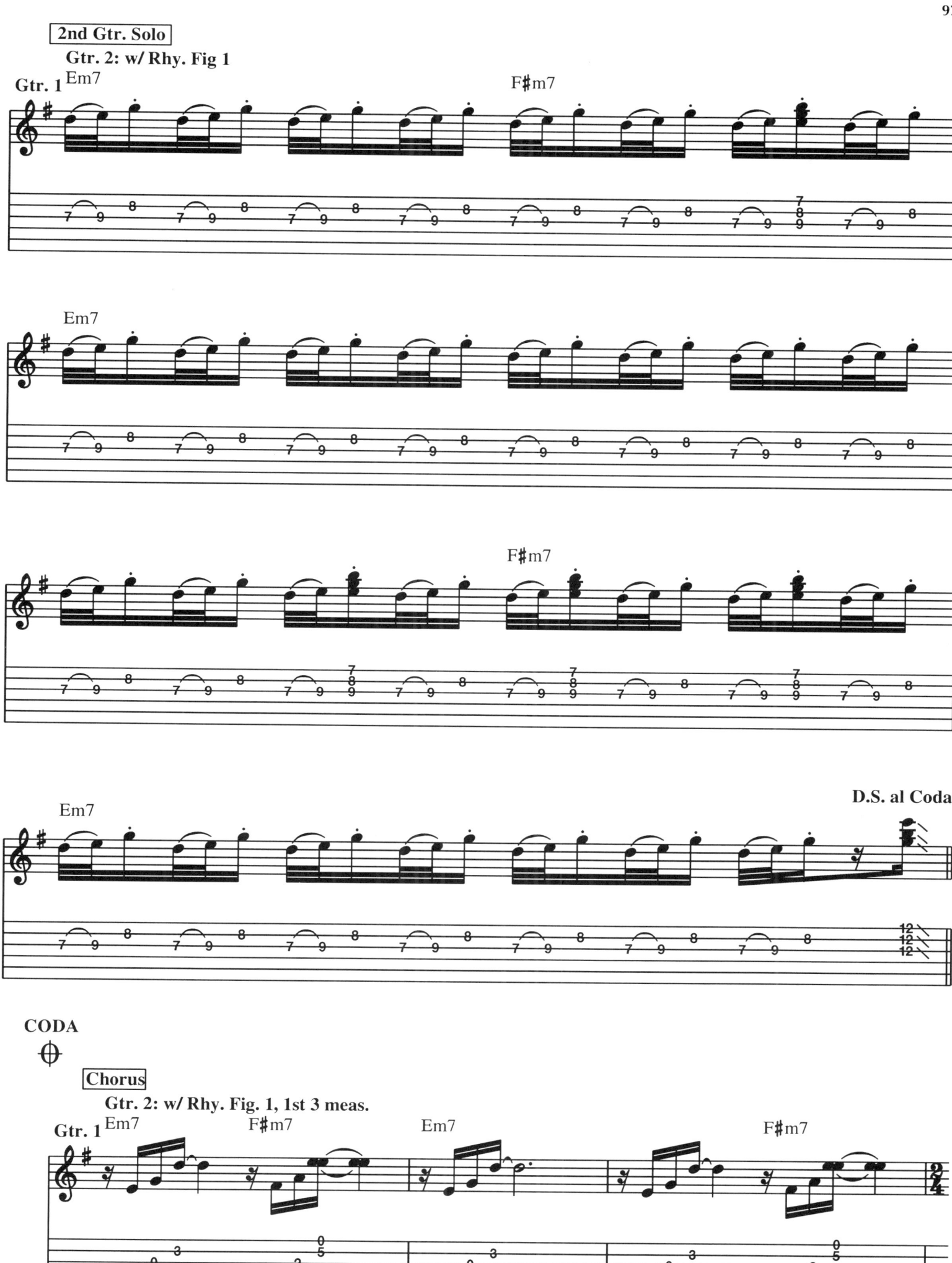

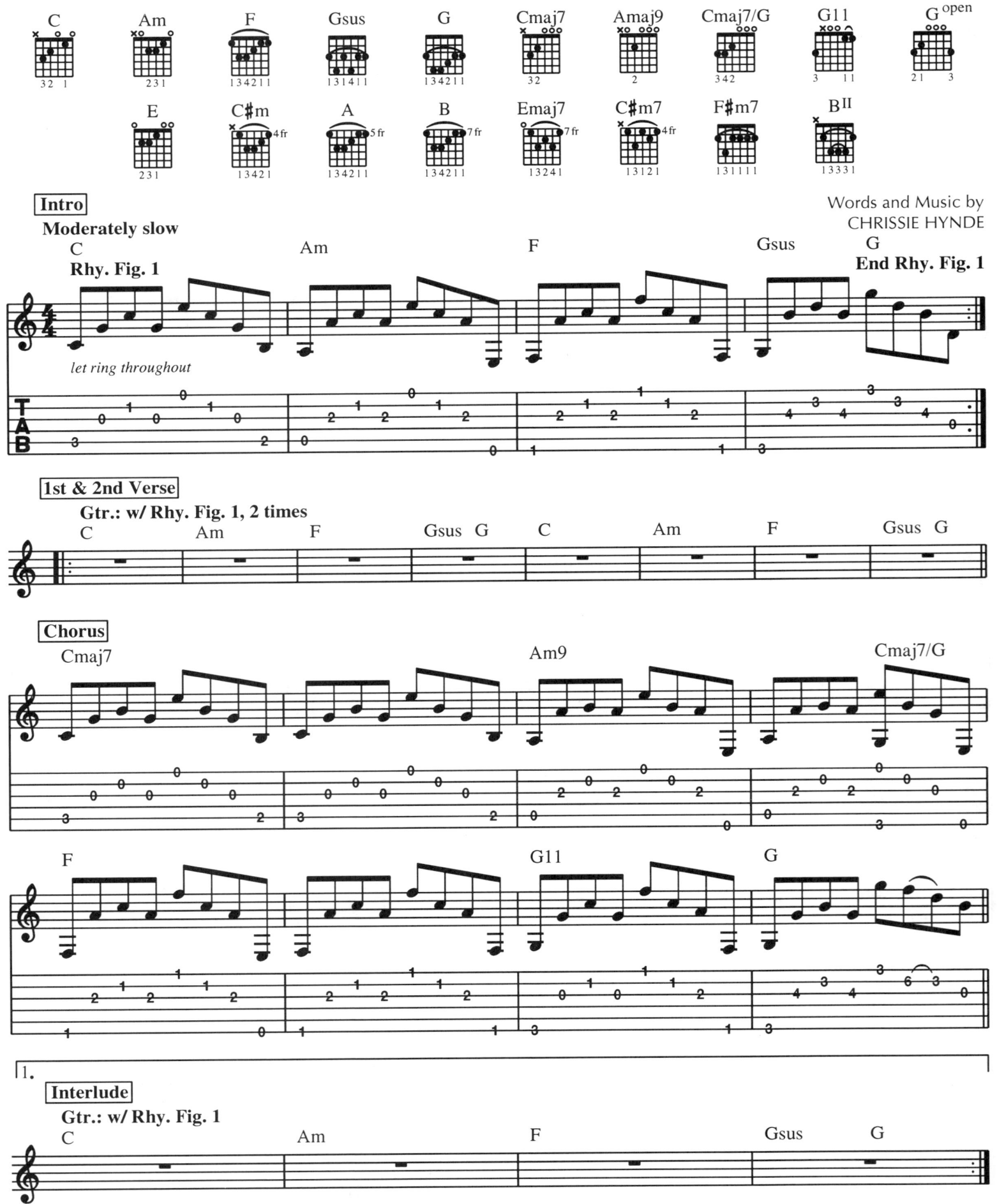

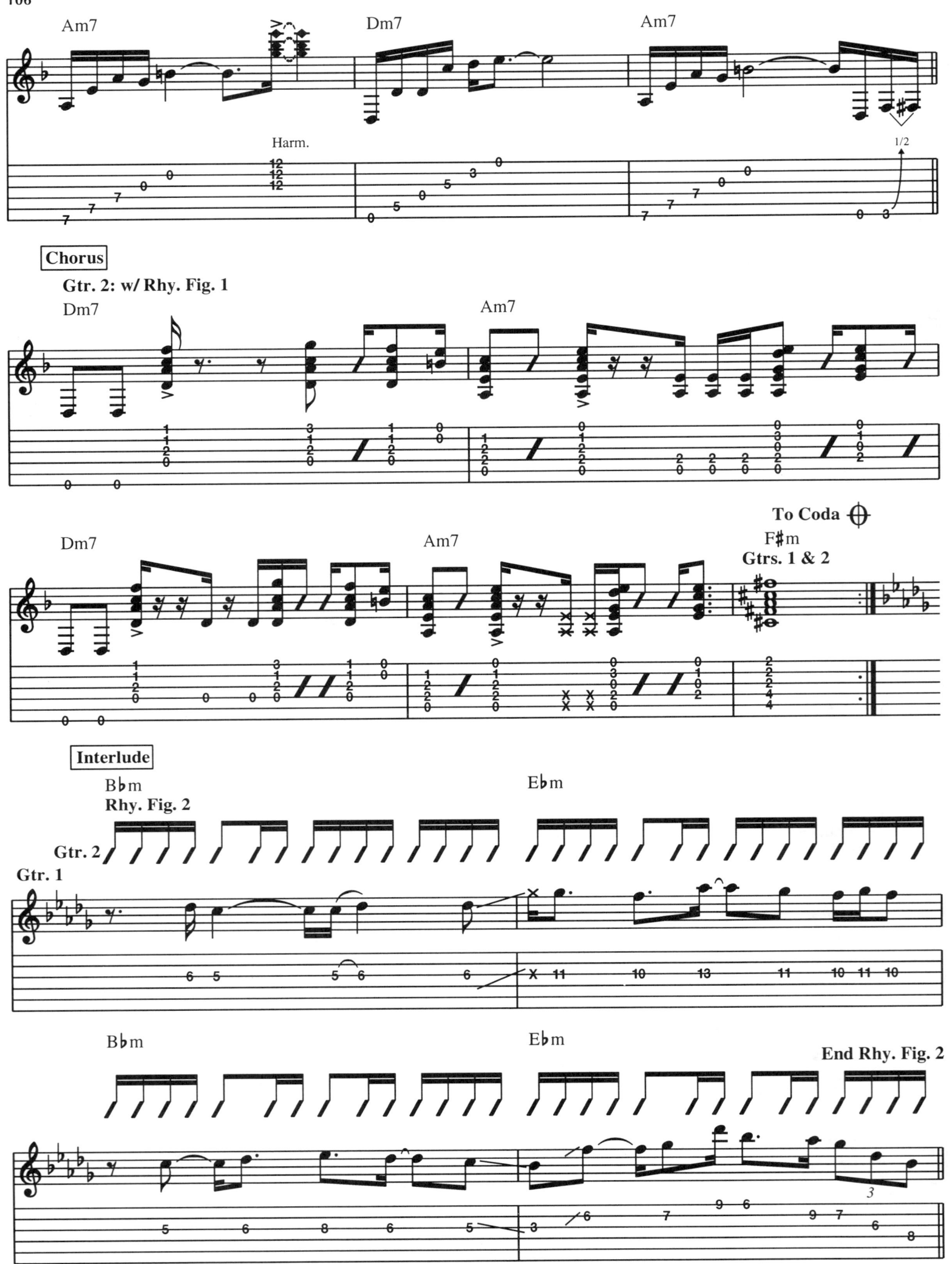

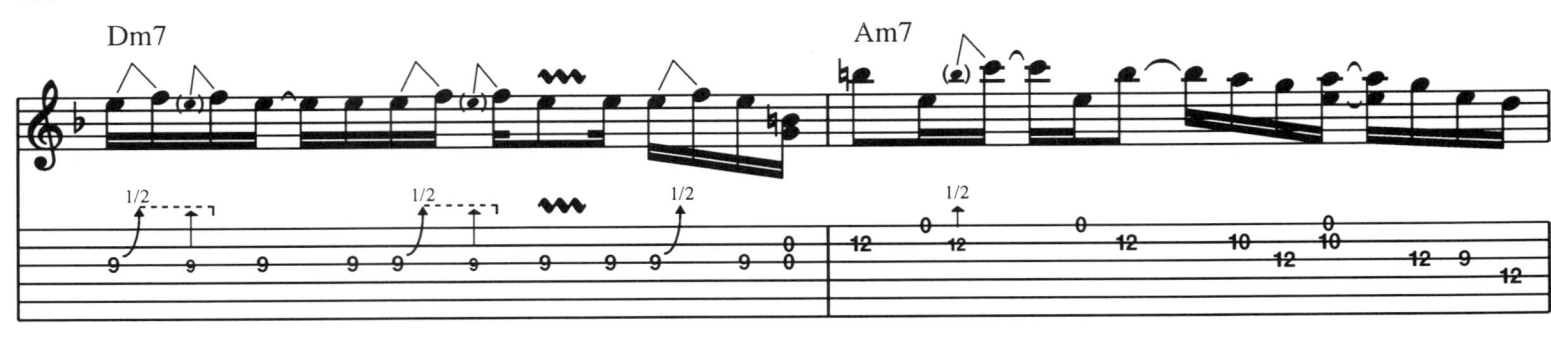

D.S. al Coda

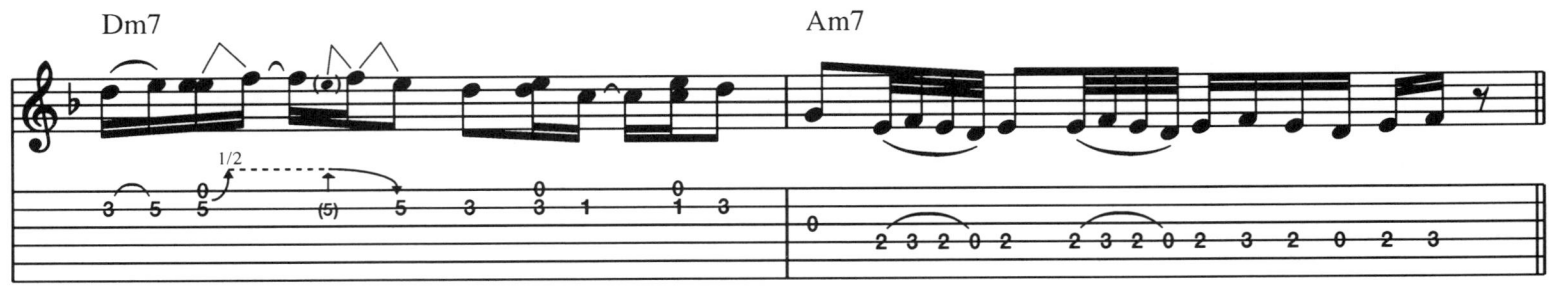

CODA

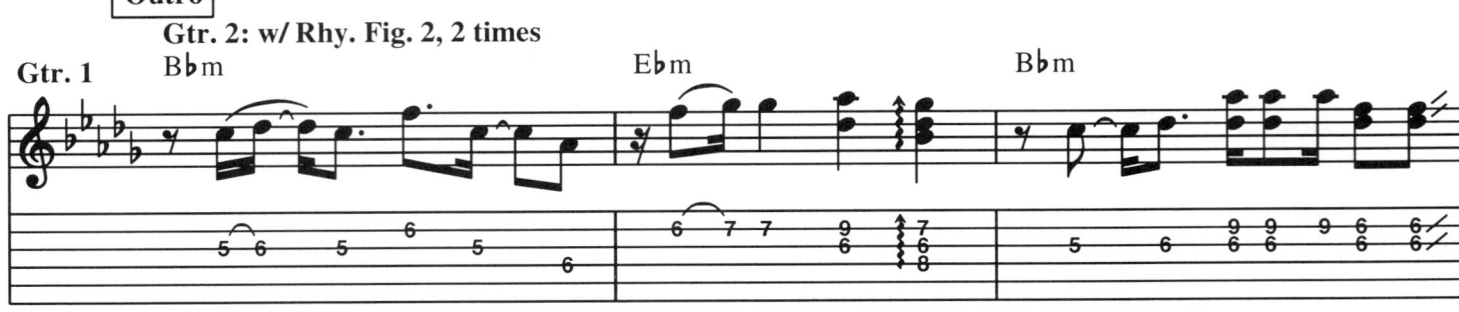

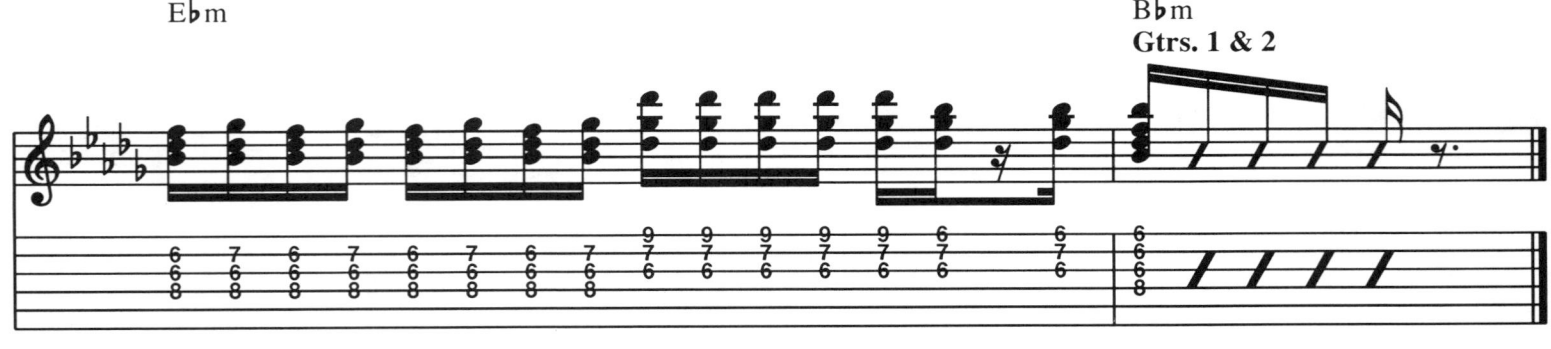

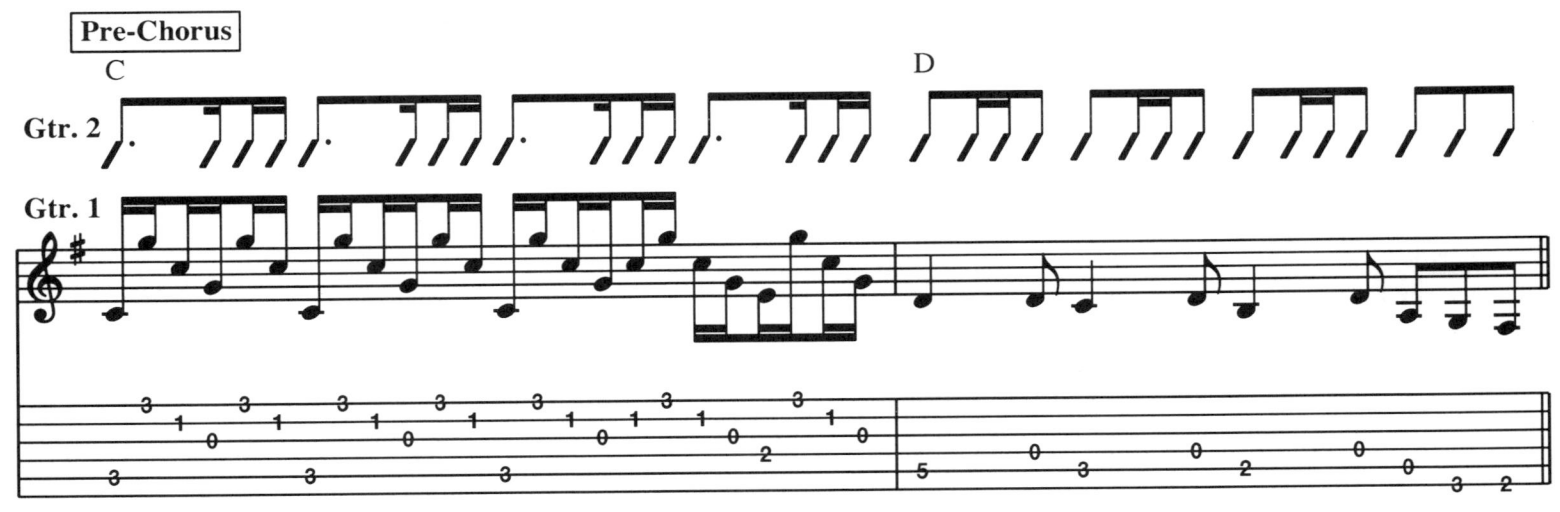
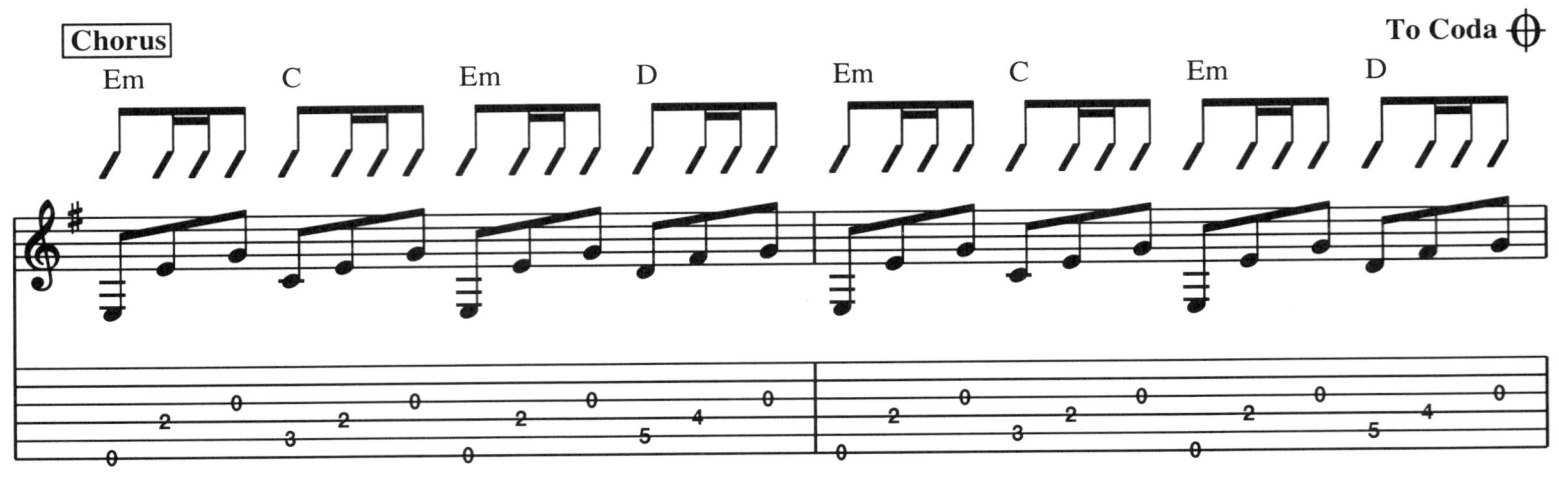
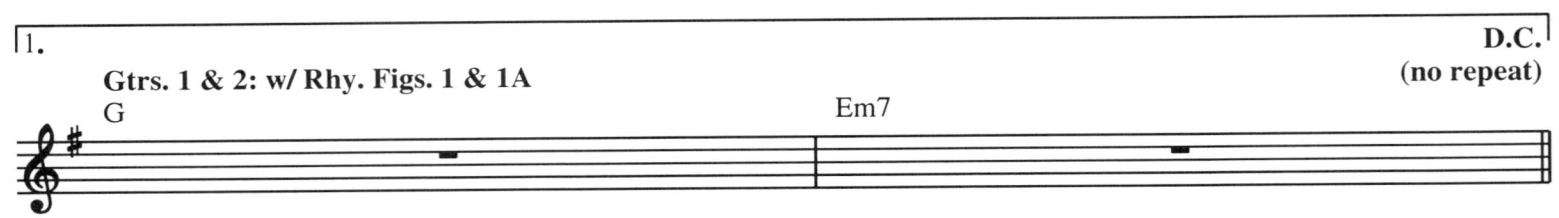
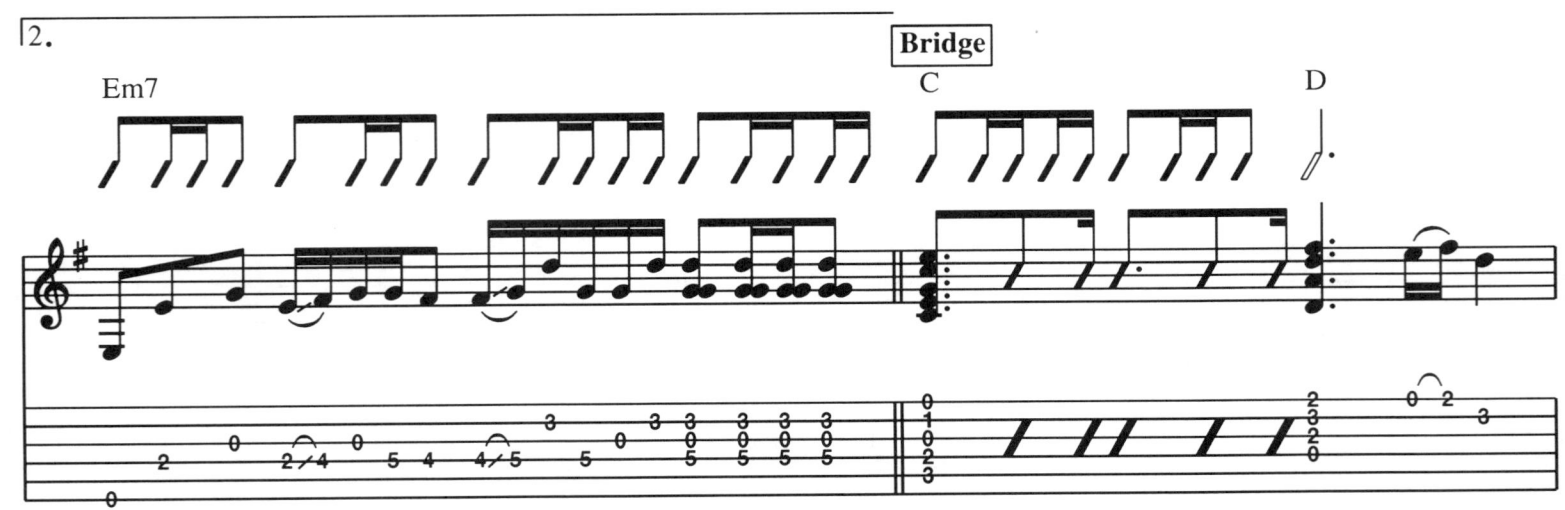

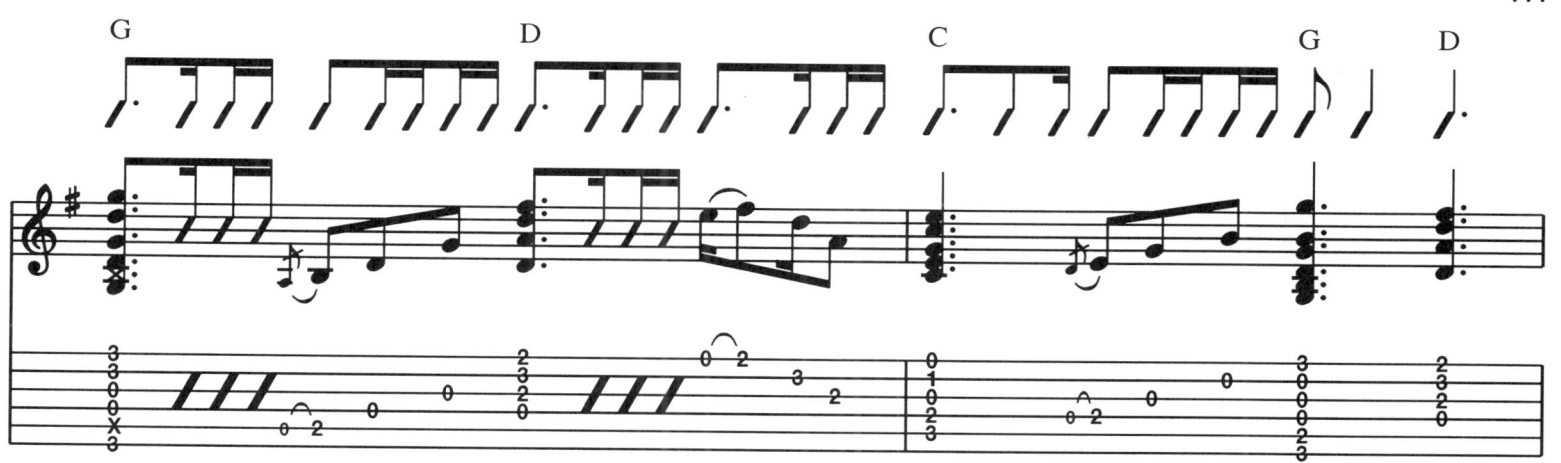
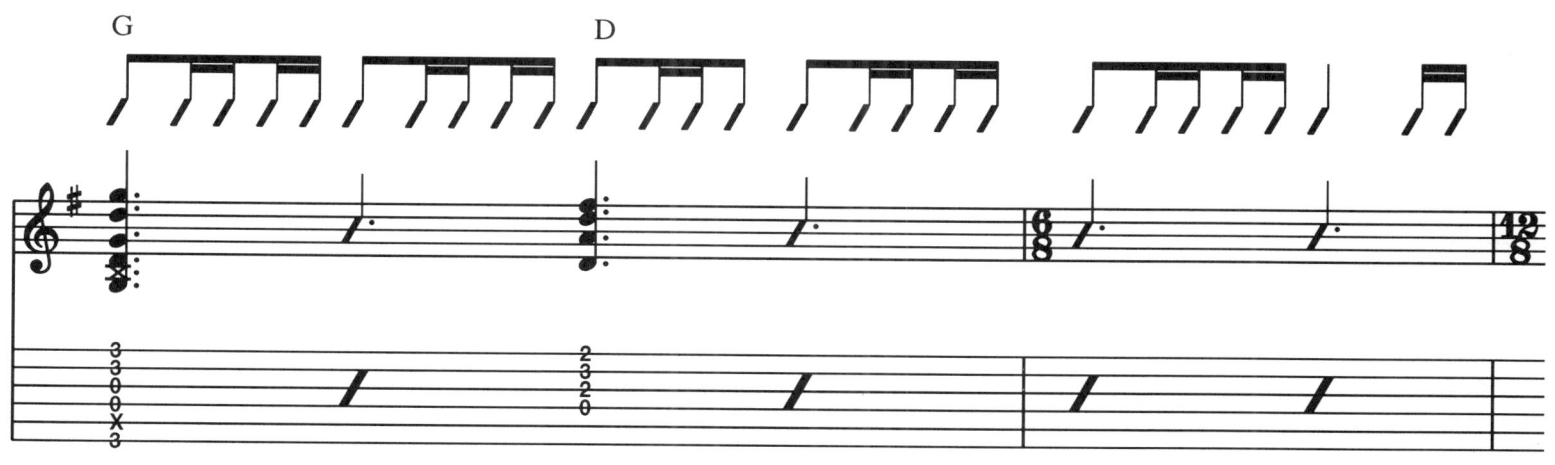

Gtr. 2: w/ Rhy. Fig. 1A, 2 times

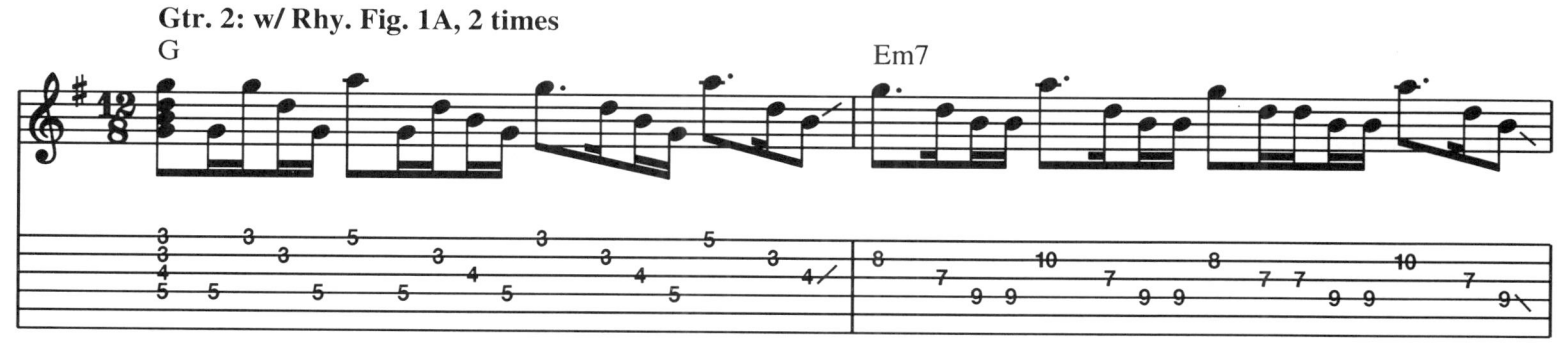
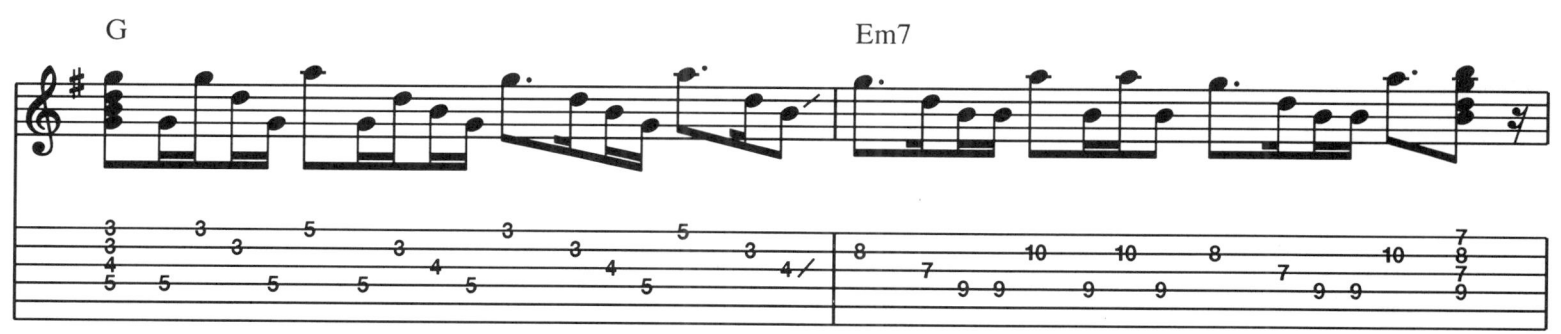

Cmaj7
D
Gtr. 2
Gtr. 1
D.S. al Coda
Cmaj7
D
CODA
Em
C
Em
D
G
D
C
D
Em7
let ring
poco rit.
Harm.

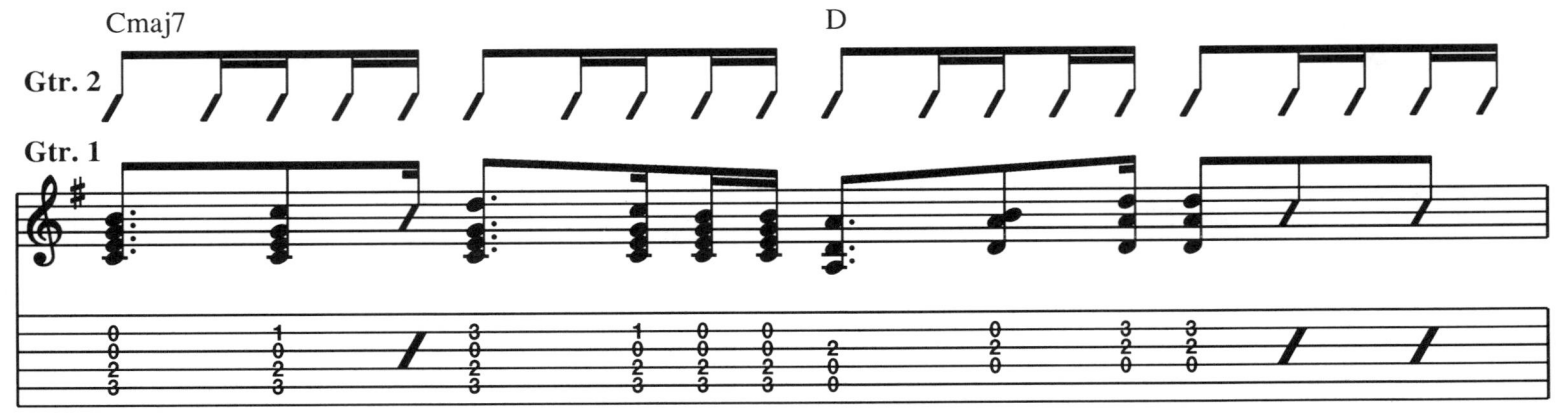

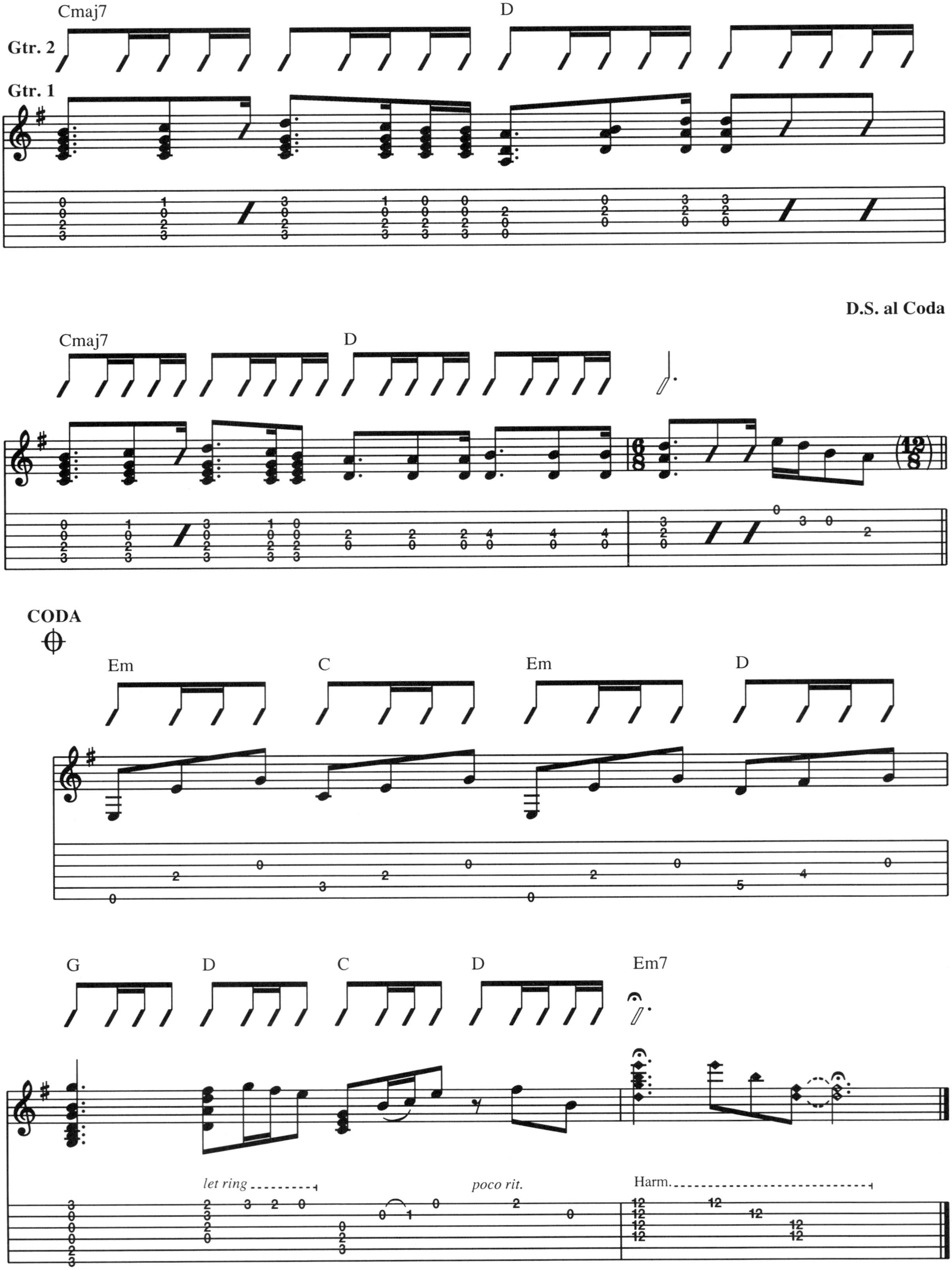

BRASS IN POCKET
(Guitar Part)

Words and Music by CHRISSIE HYNDE and JAMES HONEYMAN-SCOTT

© 1979 EMI Music Publishing LTD. trading as CLIVE BANKS SONGS and JAMES HONEYMAN-SCOTT
All Rights for EMI Music Publishing LTD. trading as CLIVE BANKS SONGS Controlled and Administered by EMI APRIL MUSIC INC.
All Rights Reserved   International Copyright Secured   Used by Permission

HYMN TO HER
(Guitar Chords)

Words and Music by
MEG KEENE

C5 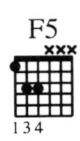   F5 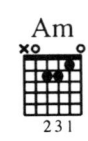   Am 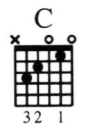   C 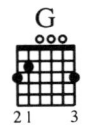   G    B♭/F

© 1986 HYNDE HOUSE OF HITS
All Rights Controlled and Administered by EMI APRIL MUSIC INC. under license from SONY/ATV TUNES LLC
All Rights Reserved   International Copyright Secured   Used by Permission

I GO TO SLEEP
(Guitar Chords)

Words and Music by
RAY DAVIES

Am    C 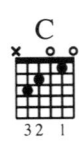   Em/B 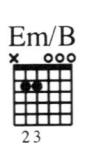   G 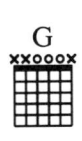   B 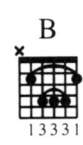   A♭ 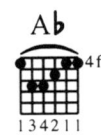   E♭ 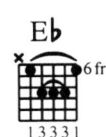   G7    Am(add9)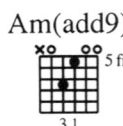

Copyright © 1965 Edward Kassner Music Co., Ltd., for the World
Copyright Renewed
Controlled in the U.S.A. and Canada by Jay Boy Music Corp.
International Copyright Secured   All Rights Reserved

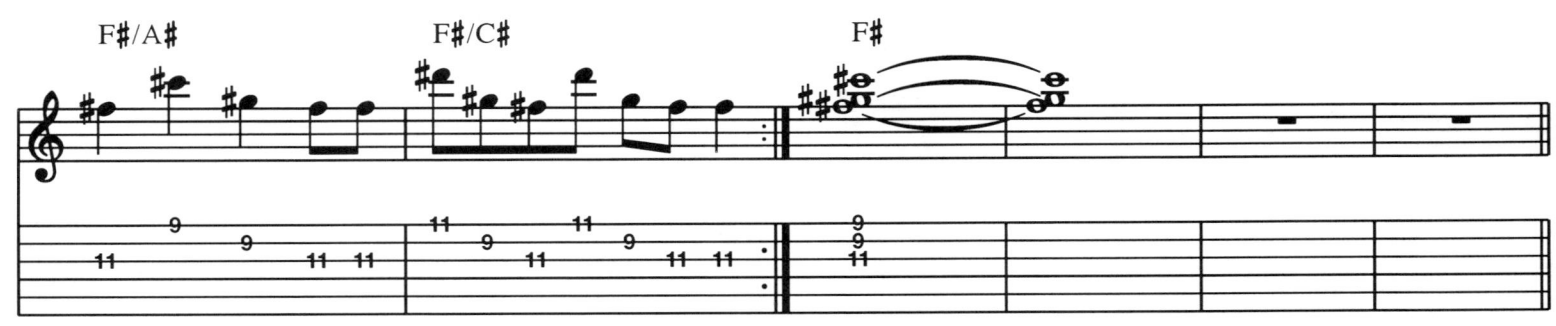

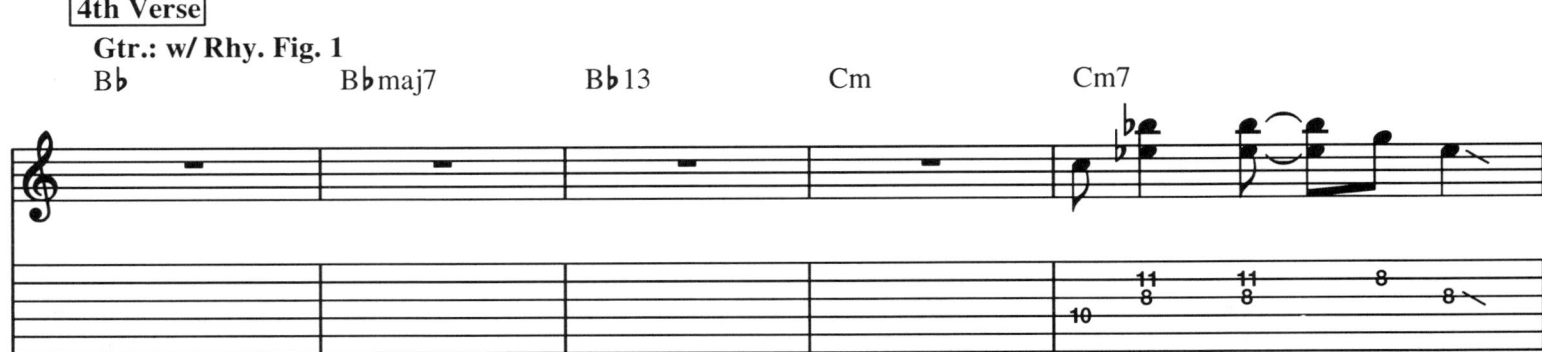

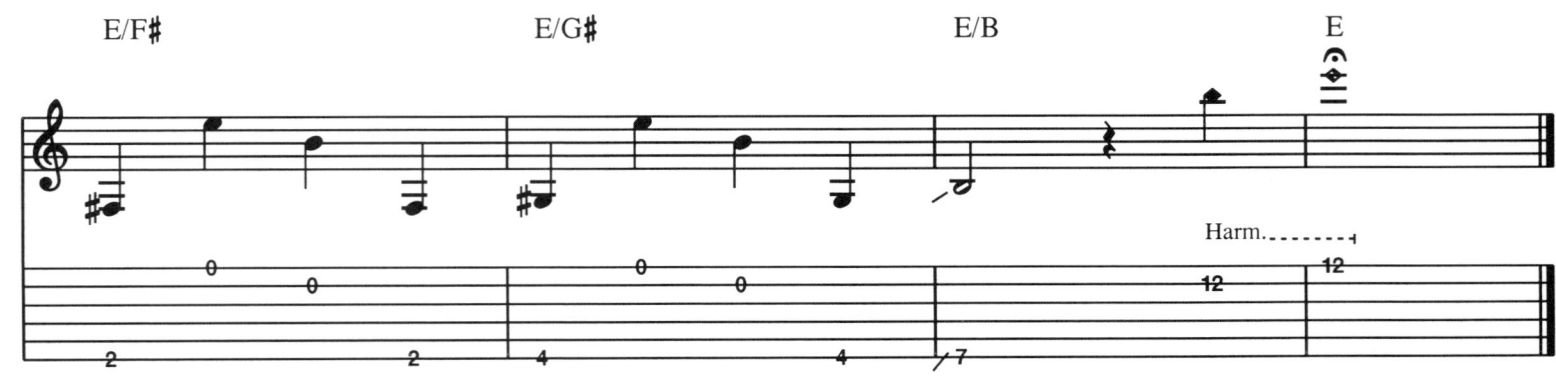

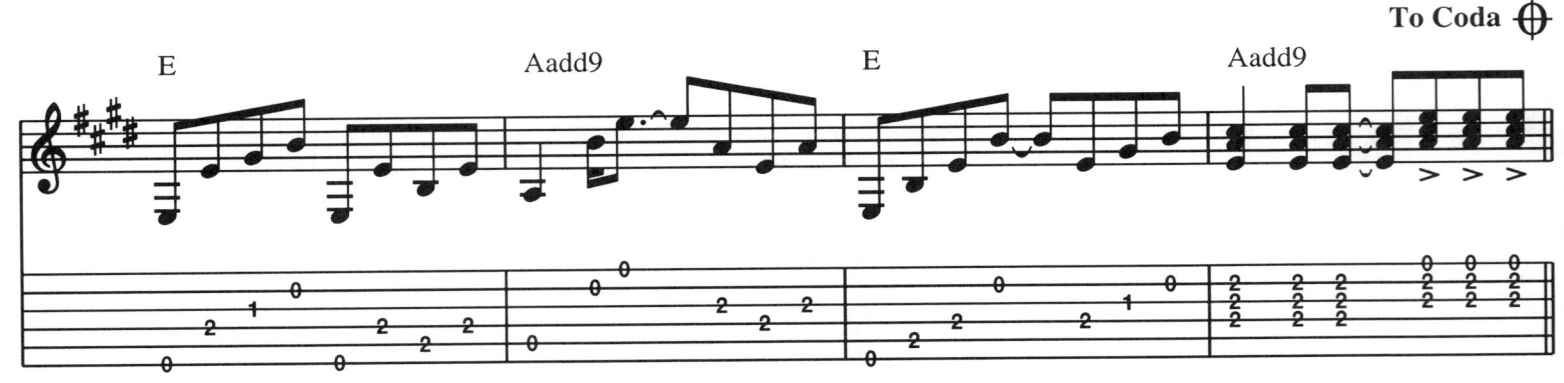